2nd Edition 2013
Published by Sifi Publishing

www.sifipublishing.co.uk

CONTENTS

LIST OF ILLUSTRATIONS

AUTHOR'S NOTE

The story in this book is one of the oldest stories of the West European peoples; a part of their basic heritage.

TRISTAN
THE LOVER

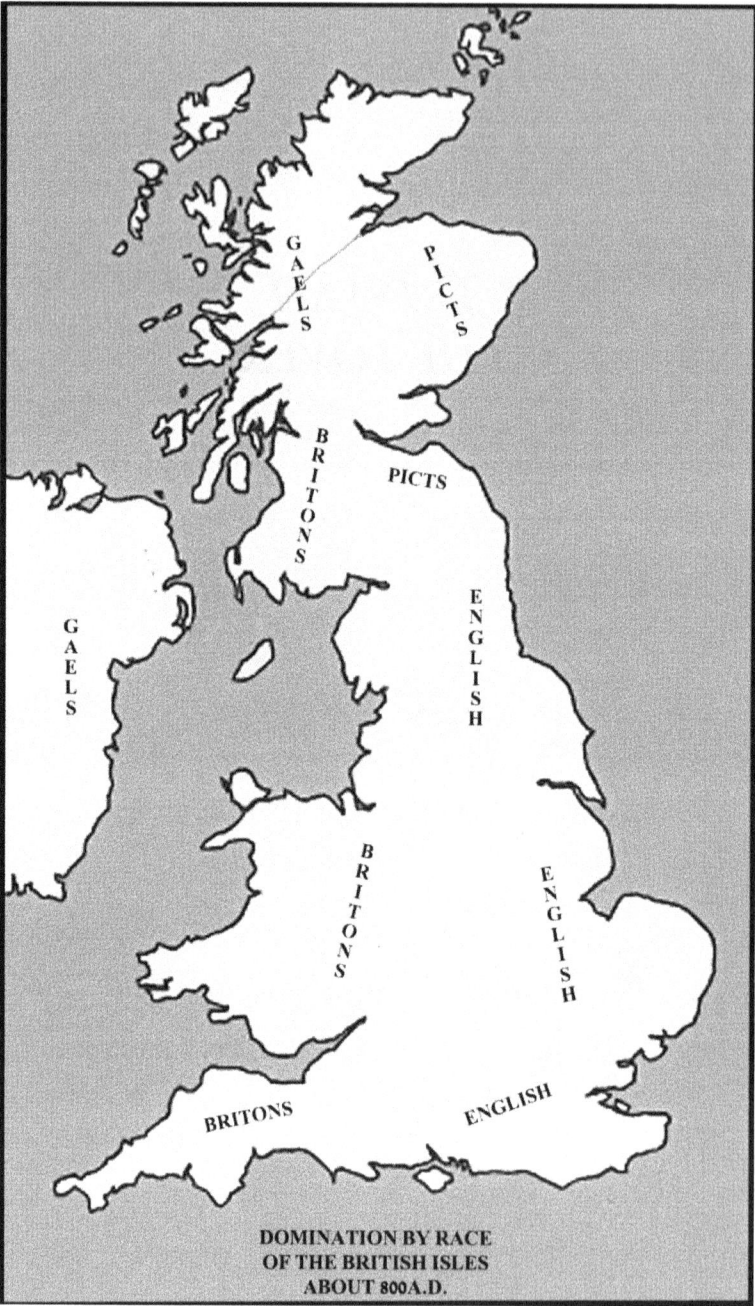

DOMINATION BY RACE
OF THE BRITISH ISLES
ABOUT 800A.D.

GAELS

PICTS

BRITONS

PICTS

GAELS

ENGLISH

BRITONS

ENGLISH

BRITONS

ENGLISH

STRATHCLYDE

LOTHIAN

NORTHUMBRIA

CUMBRIA

LEINSTER

WALES

wessex

CORNWALL

FRISIA

BRITANNY

FRANKLAND

THE KINGDOMS OF N.W. EUROPE
IN TRISTAN'S STORY

INTRODUCTION

CELTIC LEGEND

Several medieval versions of the famous story of Tristan and Isolt have survived to our day. The earliest of them dates from about 1150 A.D. but clearly the story was already old by then and it is probable that it was originally a half-historical Celtic legend.

The British Isles were inhabited chiefly by Celtic peoples, until the Teutonic peoples, the English and Vikings, gradually conquered and then settled in England, parts of Scotland and parts of Ireland. Before the earliest English settlements there were in Britain three Celtic peoples. They were (1) the Britons in England, Wales and South-West Scotland, (2) the Gaels in Ireland, Man and Western Scotland and (3) the Picts in Eastern and Northern Scotland. But in the end the Britons held out only in Wales and the Picts were overrun by the English and Gaels.

800 A.D. BACKGROUND

Both the name Tristan and the background events in his story fit the history of the British Isles about 800A.D.. At that time the Pictish kingdom of Lothian, the capital of which was probably Edinburgh, had a king and several princes called Drost or Drustan and Lothian was often invaded from the south-east by the Anglian King of Northumbria. During the same period the Britons of Cornwall and of Cumbria, who also have a part in Tristan's story, were continually attacked both by the English and by the Irish

Gaels and during the same period the Vikings began to trade and raid along all the coasts of the British Isles.

Medieval storytellers always told their stories against a background of their own times. The surviving stories of Tristan therefore show him against a background of the Age of Chivalry and they put him into clothes, armour, buildings and boats which were in use in 1150 A.D. or later. However, because the events of the story fit 800 A.D. but not 1150, I have changed the 1150 background of the minstrels into a 800 background.

I have kept almost intact the ideals and conventions which moved the characters in the medieval stories for they are the authentic thoughts and feelings of our ancestors of the early Middle Ages and unfamiliar to us. Nevertheless, we cannot yet be certain whether these motives described by minstrels late in the 12th century are entirely appropriate to Celtic Britain in 800, because our knowledge of social history at that early date is still very slight. My own guess is that Celtic Britain in 800 was still a primitive "round hut civilisation" and that its standards of living and culture were probably similar to those of tribal societies in the third world today.

The sophisticated concept of loyalty as in honour bound which appears in the Tristan stories was probably superior to the general practice in England even in 1150 and in 800, loyalty certainly depended principally on brute force and dire necessity. Two things, however, "Tristan" shows clearly. Unswerving personal loyalty was considered the greatest virtue in the Middle Ages and, though medieval life was brutish and unfavourable to love of any sort, the experience known as "being in love" was much the same then as now.

Perhaps I ought to warn you in advance that the love story of Tristan and Isolt is neither nice nor happy. It is a primitive tragedy. The lovers are conquered by their unlawful love just as surely as a fish is conquered when it swallows the hook. Their unswerving loyalty each to the other, forces them to be disloyal to every other relationship honoured and approved by their contemporaries and they are dragged down to the muddy bottom of dishonour and disgrace.

MEDIEVAL INSPIRATION

The medieval stories about Tristan which I have chiefly used in writing this book are a German poem, *Tristan,* by Gottfried of Strasburg, a Norse poem, *Tristansaga,* by Brother Robert and a French poem, *Tristan,* by Thomas of Brittany. I have also consulted four other French poems about Tristan, one by Beroul, one called *Honeysuckle* by Marie of France and two by unknown authors called *Tristan's Madness.* All seven poems were written between 1150 and 1230.

I have used two episodes from the later French prose *Tristan* but for the most part it tells an inferior story. In English there are only the rhyming *Sir Tristrem,* a much later and rougher version of Thomas' poem, and as a part of Sir Thomas Malory's famous *Morte d'Arthur,* a poor imitation of the French prose *Tristan.* I have taken nothing from those two sources.

The love-story of Tristan and Isolt contrasts so vividly with the sombre simplicity of early medieval life that it has inspired not only storytellers but many poets and artists. During the Middle Ages it was constantly retold, and inspired more artists than any other story except those of the Bible and the Christian saints. In the past two centuries it has inspired several important poems and an opera. Wagner's opera *Tristan und Isolde* is still performed and the long poems of Swinburne, Tennyson and Mathew Arnold are in most libraries.

Some of the original medieval literature which is listed above can now be read in scholarly translations but this book retells the medieval story for the general reader. The story comes to us from the medieval minstrels who recited it (probably in a sing song voice) in rich men's halls. So, even if you usually skim a text to harvest the sense of it, you may like to read this book by sounding the words in your head.

TRISTAN
THE
LOVER

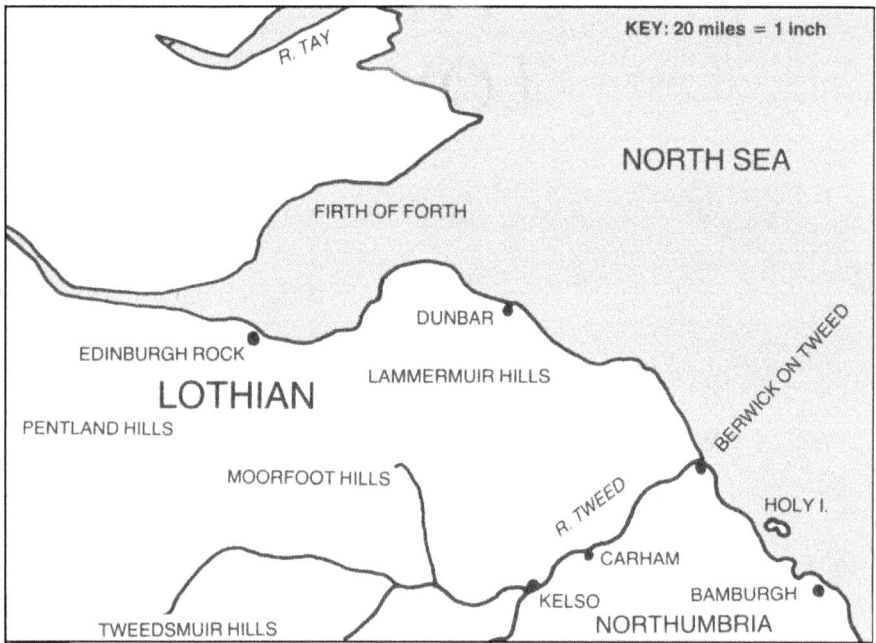

KEY: 20 miles = 1 inch

R. TAY

NORTH SEA

FIRTH OF FORTH

DUNBAR

BERWICK ON TWEED

EDINBURGH ROCK

LAMMERMUIR HILLS

LOTHIAN

PENTLAND HILLS

MOORFOOT HILLS

HOLY I.

R. TWEED

CARHAM

KELSO

BAMBURGH

TWEEDSMUIR HILLS

NORTHUMBRIA

CHAPTER 1

THE CASTAWAY

It was a very sad day in Edinburgh when Tristan was born. It was sad, not because of his birth, but because on the previous day the Picts of Lothian had been defeated by the English of Northumbria. It was especially sad, because Tulloch, the King of Lothian, had been killed in battle and because his young wife, Whiteflower, had died at the news and it was saddest of all because as a result of the defeat, the people of Lothian were again at the mercy of the Northumbrians.

The victorious English were looting the unprotected farms and the Pictish chiefs were grovelling before King Morgan of Northumbria, hoping to save their lives and lands. But amid all the fear and uncertainty the Lady Florence lay beside the newborn child in the large earth-and-timber fort on Edinburgh Rock. She held him close against her and guarded him from every doubt and dread. The Lady Florence was the wife of "Faithful Ronald," who had been right-hand man and marshal to the dead King Tulloch and it was Ronald who held the Rock, the strongest hill-fort in Lothian.

King Morgan was content to have plundered the Lothian countryside and to have taken oaths of homage from Ronald and the Pictish chiefs so he did not try to capture the Rock, before he withdrew to his own stronghold at Bamburgh.

The horrors of war and the terrors of defeat never touched the boy Tristan and he grew strong, healthy and handsome in the great fort. Although some said that his name Tristan was short for "tristis homo" meaning "sad man," Tristan the boy was untouched by sorrow because his mother, the Lady Florence, cherished him even more tenderly than she had cherished his six elder brothers. It was usual in those days for a boy to live in the women's quarters for the first seven years of his life but at the age of seven, Tristan was taken from his mother's care and put in the charge of a master. Ronald told the master to teach Tristan as much as he could before the boy became a man and he sent them abroad, in order that Tristan might learn foreign languages and the various skills of distant lands.

For seven years Tristan and his master roamed the known world and Tristan learnt every tongue that he heard and read every book that he could borrow. But the three arts at which he most excelled were the arts of music, hunting and war, for there was no stringed instrument which he could not play; there was no beast or bird which he did not know how to hunt with hawk or hound or bow or spear, and there was no type of combat either on foot, or mounted, at sea or on land, armed or unarmed, which he had not mastered. Tristan did not learn all these things without hard work and he was a serious youth but he was certainly not "tristis."

When Tristan was fourteen years old, his father called him home and sent him travelling the hills and forests of Lothian, to get to know the land and its people. Tristan performed so well at all the tasks which the Marshal set him and reported so skilfully on all that he observed, that he was rewarded with the best of everything. Tristan was better dressed, better horsed and better provided than anyone else in Ronald's hall.

Tristan's elder brothers were jealous but they soon found that, if they wanted anything, they only needed to persuade Tristan to ask his father for it and Ronald would gladly give it to him. Consequently, they gained from their father's devotion to the youth and they treated Tristan with more respect than younger brothers usually get.

"Tristan! Where are you?" Tristan heard the voice of his youngest brother and looked up from feeding his young merlin falcon. The two youngest of his elder brothers were running towards him, with the fair wisps of proud young beards blowing behind their ears.

"Tristan, there is a big ship lying in the river-mouth, a Norway trading ship driven here by storms. The harbourmaster says that the ship has a cargo of Norway goods: squirrel and marten furs, pelts of beaver and bear, walrus tusks and beeswax, cowhides and goat skins, dried fish, amber, tar, oil and pumice stone and the traders also have goshawks and falcons. The harbourmaster says that he has never seen better hunting-birds. Tristan, ask Father to buy each of us a falcon or a hawk, for you are the only one who has a bird of his own and yours is only young."

Tristan found Ronald in the grain-store, measuring with his eye the dwindling heaps of last year's corn and the Marshal was pleased, because in spite of the ravages of mice and mildew there would be enough corn to provide bread for his large household until the next harvest. When Tristan made his request, the Marshal suspected his two elder sons, but he could not refuse Tristan. He patted his shoulder and said that he himself would take them to see the ship. Ronald took Tristan's hand and the two youths who had brought the news gathered their brothers. Then all the men of the family, with Tristan's master and a numerous escort of squires and pages, rode down to the seashore.

Although the Picts used clumsy wooden boats for carrying timber, they preferred to travel in lighter, faster boats made of hazel-rods, plaited willow-wands and tanned cowhides and it was in a fleet of such skinboats that the Marshal's party rowed out to the oak-planked Norway trading ship. The Norse traders smiled and bowed, when they saw that their visitor was a great chieftain and their captain gave Ronald a ball of yellow amber. Ronald wanted to buy a rack of sable furs to trim his wife's gown but he spoke no Norse and the traders understood neither Pictish nor Gaelic nor English.

Suddenly Tristan noticed his father gesticulating with his hands and fingers, while the ship's captain shrugged his shoulders. "Perhaps I can help you, dear Father" Tristan said, and he interpreted the Marshal's words into Norse and the captain's words into Pictish. Ronald soon completed his purchase for his wife and with Tristan's help he bought a young falcon or a hawk for each of his elder sons and a big white Jeerfalcon for Tristan. Meanwhile, Tristan had become the centre of an admiring crowd of Norse seamen and traders for they had never met so young a foreigner so fluent in their language.

Ronald was already calling his boat in order to go ashore, when Tristan noticed a fine chessboard hanging by its ring above the captain's chest in the stern. He asked, "Is that chessboard for sale, Captain? Or do you traders pass the time on long sea voyages with the subtle sport of the Egyptian kings?"

"Everything in this ship is for sale at a price," the Norseman answered with a smile. "But we should not want to part with our chessmen so early in the voyage for many of us play chess and it entertains us well, when we have no work to do." Tristan said to the Marshal, "Father, I have not had a game of chess since Master and I were in Cordova. I should dearly like to play a few games with the traders."

"My son, I can see nothing against it," Faithful Ronald replied. "But I and your brothers will return to the shore with what we have bought for I have work to do before dark. Your master can stay here with you and on my behalf, you must ask the captain to give me an assurance that he will return you to the shore when you are ready to come home."

The captain promised to put Tristan ashore, as the Marshal asked and all the other Picts went home leaving only Tristan playing chess and Master watching the play. Tristan defeated first the captain and then all the other chess players in the ship's company. Later, when the traders plied him with questions in the various languages which they had picked up in their voyages, he answered each of them in the appropriate language. Tristan and Master thoroughly enjoyed the game of wits and they were flattered by the traders' admiration of Tristan's learning. From where they sat on deck under an awning they did not see the seamen quietly raising the anchor and the ship had drifted several miles on the ebb-tide and the off-shore breeze, before Tristan suddenly realised it.

Tristan's heart clenched tight with shock and he rushed to the ship's side, desperately looking for a chance to escape. But already the ship was a long way from land, too far to swim and even too far to shout to the shore. Besides, the captain said, "Don't shout;" and he put his hand on the hilt of his sword in a meaningful way.

"Why are you doing this?" Tristan asked.

"Because we want to take you with us," the captain answered.

"But what for?" Tristan asked. "I am no seaman, sir."

"A young man with such polished manners and with such a command of many languages could have a great future in trade, my boy. We want you to join our adventure. If you serve us well, you shall have a crewman's share of the profits. If not, you will fetch a high price in the slave market."

Master wailed so loudly that the seamen, instead of keeping him to sell as a slave, put him off in a boat and, although Master had never in his life rowed a boat, he made for the shore as fast as he could. But the Norsemen would not let Tristan go. They set their big, square sail and, long before Master had reached land, the ship was swallowed up in the vast expanse of the ever-moving sea and wrapped in the cloak of the impenetrable dark. When day dawned and Tristan strained his eyes to see his homeland, he saw nothing but the grey sea heaving and the grey clouds lowering above it.

The seamen jeered when they saw Tristan gazing astern and weeping and they laughed when they saw him praying to the sky. But their merriment and scornful laughter did not last long. Even as they mocked Tristan for crying to the clouds in his Christ-language, those clouds grew black. Rain whipped the men and wind clutched at them. The heavy-laden ship staggered before the storm. The leather rigging screamed and snapped, and the pine mast creaked and cracked.

"All hands to strike sail!" shouted the captain but it was doubtful whether they could lower the sail before it tore away or snapped the mast or dragged the ship under the raging sea and there were many wrenched muscles and bleeding hands before the flapping sail and the heavy mast had been stowed and lashed on the rack amidships. While the drifting ship wallowed among the mountainous waves, the captain and steersmen, two men at a time, wrestled to control the kicking steering-oar but the crew cowered beneath the gunnel with their backs turned to the stinging spray. They began to look with fear and hatred at the boy whose prayer, they thought, had brought the storm.

The fat-bellied, double-ended ship was just a big open boat with neither cabins nor any shelter other than the low gunnel and the thwarts on which the rowers sat. For a whole week she drove before the storm and for every moment of that long, long week she rolled like a drunkard. Now she pointed to the sky from the crest of a wave; now she plunged like a runaway sled into a watery ravine. Even the hardiest seaman could not stand up. So long as the men had the strength to move, they went about their tasks on hands and knees but, when they were exhausted, they bound themselves with

6

leather thongs to the thwarts and gunnel. The planking of the hull worked and groaned; the heavy cargo in the flooded bilges sloshed and thudded from side to side and the crew on deck rolled in their bonds like drowned corpses. The ale-casks were stove in; the bread and meat were sodden and briny and death seemed so inevitable that the younger sailors begged the gods to end their painful lives without delay.

As often happens when man finds himself small and weak against the full force of the elements, the Norsemen, whenever talk was possible, discussed how to obtain mercy from the gods. They were not Christians and their ancient religion sat lightly upon them but, as the days followed the nights and the nights followed the days, with neither break nor slackening in the fury of the storm, two opinions emerged. Those who were lashed to the port side of the ship thought it necessary to buy mercy from the gods with a sacrifice and they said that the only acceptable gift would be Tristan, the youngest man aboard. But those who were bound to the starboard gunnel argued that their own gods were powerless against the god who had raised the storm and they said that it would be best to make Tristan pray to his god for better weather.

These two opinions were passed to the quarterdeck, where, lashed to the ship, lay the captain, his three assistant steersmen and the two traders who had put up the money for the expedition. The men on the quarterdeck had no book-learning but they had seen many lands. They were doubtful whether sacrifices or gifts had much influence with the gods. Therefore, when the port watch suggested that Tristan should be thrown overboard in order to appease the angry gods, the leaders frowned and shrugged uncertainly and they listened more favourably when the starboard watch proposed that Tristan should be ordered to pray to his god for better weather. The traders had heard that Christians and Moslems believed that wrongdoing is punished by the One God and they thought that the One God had punished them with the storm because the captain had broken his word by abducting Tristan.

By good fortune Tristan heard enough of the discussion on the quarterdeck to understand it, because at the very beginning of the week-long storm he had crawled into the little triangular cave in the stern where the ship's sides fitted into the sternpost. Every waking hour he had been asking God to halt the storm for he was both scared and painfully sick with the incessant noise and movement of the storm-racked ship. But he was more sheltered in his little cave than anyone else aboard and the captain had given him his share of whatever food and ale was handed round. Therefore Tristan was not too fuddled to realise that he might strike a bargain with his captors. He obstinately refused to pray to the One God, unless the Norsemen promised to put him ashore as a free man as soon as they saw land.

Now Tristan was only a fifteen-year-old youth among thirty hardened and well-armed seamen but he alone knew the language of the One God and many of the seamen believed that it was the One God who controlled this storm. Therefore the captain, after consulting his men, agreed to Tristan's terms.

"You broke your word to my father because you promised to put me ashore in Edinburgh," said Tristan. "How can I be sure that you will keep your word this time?"

"We will swear both on Thor's 'T' and on Odin's ring," said the captain; "for Thor and Odin are the chief of our gods."

"They are not gods in whom *I* believe," Tristan pointed out. "I should rather that we shook hands upon our agreement for whoever breaks his word after shaking hands upon it is an outcast among men in every land."

Therefore the captain repeated the agreement and shook hands with Tristan and after the captain, everyone on the quarterdeck did the same. Then Tristan put his hands together palm to palm and turned his face to the weeping sky, and he prayed aloud in Latin: *"A fulgure et tempestate libera nos, Domine"* "From lightning and storm deliver us, O Lord"

Over and over again Tristan prayed that prayer. First the rain stopped; next the gale abated; then the clouds lifted and at last the angry white caps vanished from the rolling waves.

The seamen untied their bonds and laughed with joy to find themselves still alive and they cut the lashings with which they had secured the steering-oar and the mast and sail. They were already stepping the mast in its housing and wedging it in place with the mast-fish, when a glad cry sang out from the prow: "Land-ho! Land-ho! Land on the starboard bow!"

The captain had seen neither land nor sun nor stars for the past week, while his ship had been driven along in the all-enshrouding darkness of the tempest. He knew only that from the Firth of Forth they had been driven far to the South. Now, therefore, he pushed the others aside and climbed the mast, eager to see the land which had been reported. However, when he came down, he shook his head in disappointment.

"A most unfriendly coast" he told the steersman. "And I do not recognise it. Only Tristan's god knows where he has brought us. Nevertheless, steer towards the shore and prepare a boat. We must keep our word to Tristan first. We can find our bearings later."

"Sir, don't put me ashore on an unknown coast," Tristan begged. "It may be uninhabited or the home of trolls or robbers or man-eating beasts."

"We shook hands on an agreement to put you ashore as soon as we saw land," said the captain. "And there it is."

The captain pointed ahead to where the massive waves of the storm-driven sea were smashing themselves against a ragged line of gaunt grey cliffs and, when he had brought his waterlogged ship as near as he dared to the rocky coast, he gave orders to lower the boat. Tristan was given a leather wallet containing some sodden bread and some smoked meat and he was rowed ashore into a sheltered cove.

"The gods give you good day!" the Norsemen cried and they left Tristan on a narrow strip of sand between the sheer cliffs and the turbulent sea. But there were only screaming sea birds to welcome him. Small wonder that Tristan sat down and cried! Small wonder that, even though the shipmen had not been his friends, he held onto their ship with his eyes, until she had sailed from his sight!

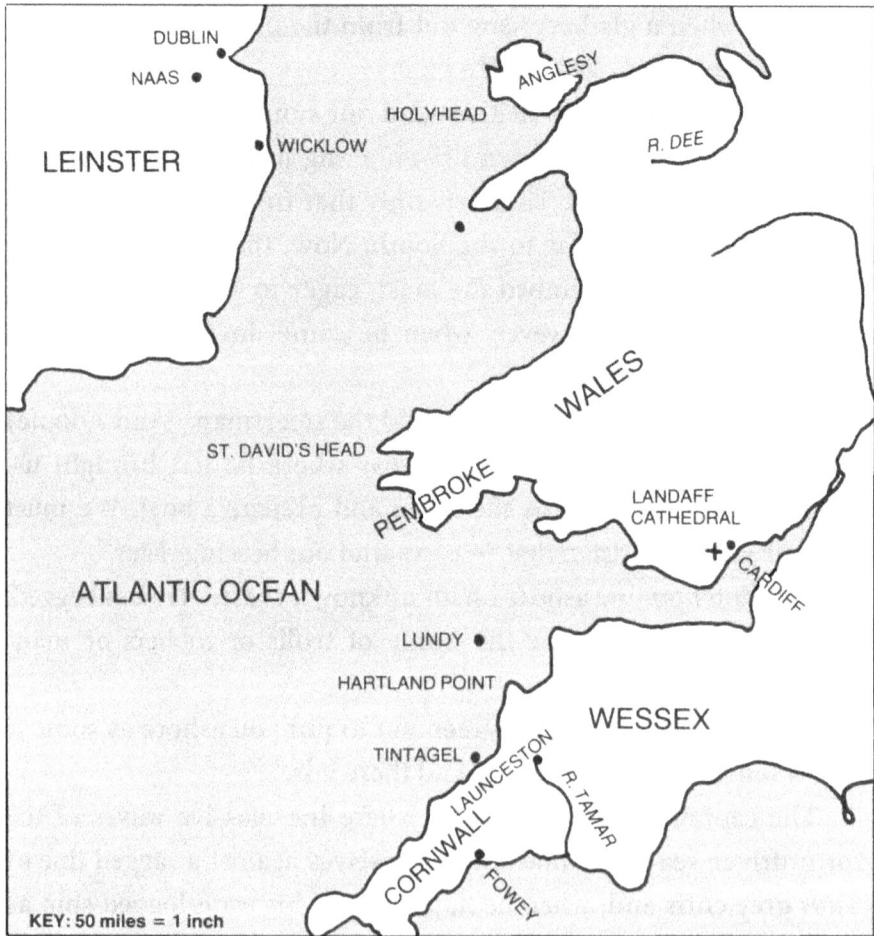

CHAPTER 2

THE KING'S SQUIRE

Tristan looked around him. The cliffs towered above him and walled him in on the landward side. He gazed in terror at the storm-roused sea, hurling its massive waves to steaming destruction on the headlands which guarded the bay. Fear gripped his heart when he noticed that even inside the sheltered cove the huge waves sprang upon the sandy shore as if trying to swallow it. He gave up hope and he closed his eyes and prayed.

"Save me, O God!" he cried helplessly. "I do not know in what land I am nor whether its people are good or evil nor whether it is a hunting ground for savage beasts. I can see nothing but impassable cliffs and impassable sea but Thou, O Lord, Thou knowest the road to safety."

At that moment Tristan felt his feet grow suddenly cold. He looked down and saw with horror that the ravening sea was snatching at him with greedy claws. The tide was coming in and coming quickly. Terror drove him to find a way to save his life. He rushed at the cliff and seized a handhold here and a foothold there, and he scrambled up the rock face until he had reached a narrow ledge above the high tide mark.

Then Tristan thanked God for saving his life, and from his own sorrows he turned his mind to the sorrows of his family and friends in Lothian. *For,* he thought, *they do not know whether I am alive or dead, freeman or slave, on sea or on land. They do not know where in the world I am nor whether indeed I am still in this world.*

When Tristan thought of his father and mother praying for him, he felt the strength of their prayers; his courage returned to him and, with eager eyes, he searched for a way up the face of the cliff. He saw that the sun was already past its midday height and he started climbing, in order to reach some safer lodging before dark.

By the time that Tristan had reached the top of the soaring wall of rock, the sun was setting and he was bruised, bloody, and very tired. He therefore hurried across the open grassland on the cliff tops and hid himself in a small valley, where bushes and brambles grew thickly beside a tumbling stream. He made himself a bed of bracken in a dry cave beneath a jutting rock, curled up in his plaid, and fell asleep.

In the morning Tristan rejoiced to find himself out of sight of the sea, with its daunting memories of the stormy voyage and he ate the food given him by the Norsemen. Feeling more cheerful, he set out inland. He wanted to avoid meeting anyone in such a lonely place, for he knew that men are always readier to do wrong when no one is looking than when they are in a crowded place and so far as possible he kept hidden in the wooded valleys. But soon he came upon a well-trodden pathway, where he could see both hoof-marks and the ruts of chariot wheels.

Tristan chose himself a vantage point where he could see the road in both directions. He spread his chequered plaid, mauve tunic and yellow shirt on a rock, to dry them in the sun and he lay down on the springy grass in a sheltered hollow to let the sun soak into his bones. But the sun was so warm and the air was so balmy that he fell asleep.

Tristan was awakened by the sound of voices on the road below him. When he looked down from his hiding place, he found himself staring straight into the eyes of two old men for, as they were walking along the road, they had seen his clothes spread out on the hillside. Tristan and the two old men eyed each other warily for in those days there were so many landless and lawless men roaming the countryside that even poor travellers were afraid of being murdered for their clothes.

At last the old men crossed themselves and called in Latin: "God give you good luck, friend!"

"May He always have you in His keeping!" Tristan answered also in Latin, and he crossed himself— head and breast, both shoulders and belly.

Tristan and the old men took comfort at hearing Latin spoken for only churchmen and a very few educated people could speak it. The two old men were poorly dressed, with neither shoes nor any weapons except their staffs. They told Tristan that they were pilgrims who had just worshipped at Saint Michael's Mount. Tristan did not like to admit that he was a stranger in the land, because a stranger who had neither family nor friends to avenge his injury was almost certain to be robbed and either enslaved or killed. Therefore, he did not ask what country this was. He told the pilgrims that he had been parted from his friends while out hunting.

"Can you tell me where we are?" he asked.

"Well, young man!" the pilgrims answered, "We do not live here but we have been told that this road leads to Tintagel, where King Mark has his hall."

"That is where I am going, good masters," Tristan said quickly. "May I have your company on the way?"

"Certainly, good youth!" the pilgrims said and the three of them began to walk northwards along the road. As they walked, they talked of many lands and told tales of great men and miraculous holy relics. The two pilgrims were much impressed by Tristan's good clothes and even more so by his wide knowledge of distant countries. But Tristan avoided showing his ignorance of the country in which they actually were, and he told them very little about himself.

During the afternoon the travellers heard the sound of hunters' horns in the woods at the foot of the moors. Suddenly a hart, spent and breathless with long running, staggered from the woods beside the road and was pulled down and killed by hounds. Huntsmen dragged the dogs from the carcase and turned the dead deer onto all fours. Then the chief huntsman raised his sword as though to cut off the noble beast's head with its proud antlers of ten points.

"Stop, Master! In God's name, stop!" Tristan shouted in dismay. "What are you doing? That is not the right way to break up a noble hart of ten."

The chief huntsman looked up in surprise and said rather crossly, "I am breaking the beast into its four quarters, boy, in the same way as usual. I shall cut off the head, split the beast's back from neck to tail and cut the carcase into four equal parts."

"We undo a hart better where I come from," Tristan insisted, for he had forgotten the need for caution in his anxiety to see this fine beast properly flayed and divided.

The huntsman thought that Tristan looked and spoke like a chieftain's son and he thought that he might either learn some new skill from this foreigner or at least have a good laugh. So with mock humility he bowed and said, "Sir, here is the beast, untouched by any blade. Please show us your skill. We will obey your orders and lend you a hand, while you undo the beast for us."

Tristan then took leave of the pilgrims, hung his plaid on a bush, tucked up the skirts and sleeves of his tunic and tied his hair in bunches behind his ears. With the huntsmen's help he laid the hart on its back, so that he could remove the hide. First he cut from the muzzle down the centre of the chest and belly to the beast's slot. Then he stripped each of the four legs, the quarters, shoulders, flanks and the back, until the hide was flayed entirely from the carcase and laid out on the grass. Finally Tristan divided the carcase according to the rules which he had learnt and he laid the thirty two proper portions in a pile beside the hide.

"There, sir!" said Tristan, sitting back on his heels and wiping his hands on the grass. "There you have the undoing, according to the way which I was taught in Charlemagne's forests. Now you can proceed with the quarry and the present."

"God bless you, young sir!" replied the chief huntsman, shaking his head admiringly. "We know no more of the 'quarry' or the 'present' of which you speak than we did of your way of 'undoing' a deer. What do you mean by those terms?"

"The 'quarry' means the ceremonial feeding of the hounds from the beast's hide, sir and the 'present' means the same as 'the fork.' "

The huntsmen still looked puzzled and they shifted from one foot to the other like pupils before their master. "Good sir!" said their chief, "please show us   the 'quarry' or 'feeding' and the 'present' or 'fork', for we have no knowledge of such ceremonies."

Tristan cut up and threw onto the hide various parts of the beast's innards and he made the huntsmen place the hart's limbs and its head around the hide in the positions which they had occupied in life. Then he told the huntsmen to make the hounds bay at the hart's head and to let them eat up all the flesh and blood spread on the hide. "For in this way," he said, "the hounds learn that the killing of a hart is followed by a good meal and in future they will be more eager to run your game down, in order to obtain their reward." Then Tristan cut a forked branch and spitted on the fork the daintiest parts of the meat and he told the huntsmen to carry the fork of meat home to their lord and to present it with the proper ceremony.

"Lord bless you, sir!" cried the chief huntsman. "You have shown us so much that is new that we must ask you to teach us also the art of presentation. Come with us to the King's court and tell us what to do."

"Very well!" said Tristan. "Lend me a horse and a small horn which a boy can blow and remember that, whatever I sound on my horn, you must repeat it after me."

So the hunters mounted and rode home with Tristan. They rode northwards over wind-swept downs and forded rushing streams in sharp-cut, shady ravines, until, at last, they came in sight of the sea. The bare downs were so open that the few thorn-trees which had kept a hold in the shallow earth were bent and blackened by the strong sea-breeze and there was not a house, nor any living thing to be seen except a small stone church and a flock of sheep grazing on the cliff-top. But the hunters rode down from the windy downs into a steep-sided, sloping valley. Tristan saw that there were crops and apple trees in this sheltered valley and that the stream had been dammed to make a reservoir of clear, fresh water. At the foot of the valley, where the stream tumbled into a bay, there was a large camp with two long halls and many round huts made of stone and turf.

"What is this splendid city?" Tristan asked politely, although he had seen many finer towns.

"This is Tintagel, King Mark's dun, young man, and from this dun he rules the Kingdom of Cornwall, as far as the River Tamar," the chief huntsman answered proudly.

"We cannot enter so fine a place in this unruly manner," said Tristan. "I suggest that you should make your men ride in couples and carry your game in proper order."

"What do you mean, young handsome?"

"I mean that your men should carry first the noble beast's head, with its attire of antlers to the front. Then they should carry the breast, the forequarters, the ribs and the hindquarters and last of all they should carry the hide and hold aloft the fork for presentation. By your leave, good master, you and I should ride last in the procession, for you are the chief and I can act as your groom."

When the cavalcade entered the fenced yard of the King of Cornwall's palace, Tristan began to blow 'the home-coming' on his horn and, as well as they could, the other hunters followed his example. Everybody in the palace ran towards the music, for never before had they known the hunters to use such ceremony, and the King himself came to the door of his hall. The King was a tall, distinguished man of about the same age as Tristan's father and, as soon as Tristan saw him, his heart took to him. To honour the King, Tristan sounded his horn with such a series of shakes and flourishes that his companions could not follow him. Then he dismounted, to hold the chief huntsman's horse and he made the huntsman go on one knee to present the fork to King Mark.

"Who is this boy?" the King asked sternly, for he trusted no one.

The chief huntsman told the King all that Tristan had done and he told him that Tristan had said that he was the son of a merchant of Lothian. "But for my part, Sire," the huntsman added, "I can hardly believe it for this boy is so skilled in woodmanship that a merchant would have had neither the time nor the means to train him so well."

The King sent four pages to bring Tristan to him and when Tristan knelt before him, the King admired his curly brown hair and smooth white skin and full red lips. King Mark thought that Tristan was likely to be both strong and agile when he was full grown and he took to Tristan as quickly as Tristan had taken to him.

"What is your name, my friend?" asked the King.

"Tristan! God save you, Sire!"

"May God keep you too, boy!"

"Sire, may the Good Lord have both you and all your household forever in His care!"

"Tristan, I have a wish which you can grant, if you please."

"Sire, your wishes are to me commands." Tristan answered humbly.

"Then you must stay with me and be my personal huntsman. Whenever I go hunting, I want you to conduct the hunt in the excellent manner which you have been taught and I want you to teach me and my huntsmen your art of woodmanship."

A few days later the King received word that a huge hart, big and fat before the mating season, had been sighted in a wood not far away and the King rode out with his hunters and hounds and with Tristan beside him. When they had reached the edge of the wood downwind of the hart, King Mark said to Tristan: "Now, Tristan, take charge of the hunt and place your hounds and your beaters where you think best."

But Tristan answered, "By your leave, Sire, that would be unwise for I know nothing of this country, whereas your huntsmen know both the lie of the land and the habits of the deer. But, if you wish it, Sire, once the beast has been hunted and killed, I will show you how I was taught to undo a noble hart."

At the end of the day King Mark was well pleased with the hunting lore which Tristan had shown him and he commanded that every hunter in Cornwall should do his best to follow the woodmanship and the ceremonies which Tristan used.

That evening a Welsh harper played before the King and, even as the harper began to pluck his harp, Tristan cried joyfully, "Aha! The Breton lay of Gurun and his lady."

The harper said nothing and he played and sang his song to the end. But, when he had laid his harp on the ground, he asked Tristan, who was sitting at his feet, "How did you know so soon what song I would sing and where that song comes from, my child? Have you been taught it?"

"Yes, master harper," Tristan answered. "There was a time when I had some lessons on the harp and could play that lay but it is a long while since I played it."

"Please me by playing, dear child," the harper said. "Here! Take my harp and play us a little tune or sing us a little song, whichever you prefer."

Tristan was shy to take the harp, but the moment that he felt it in his hands, he forgot about the people who were around him. He shut his eyes; his fingers raced over the strings and he sang in a clear, high voice the songs of many lands. On and on he played, until every man in Tintagel had crowded into the hall to hear him, for word went round that an angel was singing in King Mark's hall. "Who is this child?" they whispered in wonder. "What page is this who can teach woodmanship to the best huntsmen and who outplays the finest harpers?"

When at last Tristan noticed the crowd around him, he laid down the harp and looked bashfully at his feet but King Mark asked him: "Can you play any other musical instrument?"

"No, Sire!" Tristan answered, blushing.

"Tristan, if you love me, tell me the truth. What else can you play?"

"Sire, since you insist, I must tell you that I have tried to learn every stringed instrument which I have come across and I can in some degree play the fiddle and the hand-organ, the harp and the rote, the lyre and the lute. Yet I can play none of them as well as I should like, for I have been playing for less than seven years."

King Mark nodded his head in approval. Then he said: "Tristan, I noticed that you sang songs in several tongues. I think that I heard Breton, Welsh, Gaelic, good Latin and Frankish and I heard other tongues which I did not recognise. Can you speak all those languages?"

Tristan blushed and looked at his feet but he told the truth. "Yes, Sire!" he said, "I can both speak and read fairly well in all those languages."

Just as had happened in the Norsemen's ship, so in King Mark's court whoever had a smattering of any foreign tongue pressed forward, to question Tristan and very politely Tristan answered each question in the language in which it was asked. But after a while King Mark sent his men away. "For Tristan is only a young boy," he said. "We must not tire him out. There will be many other days for you to talk to him in any language you like. But now I want to ask him something important."

The King turned to Tristan and took his hand. 'Tristan!" he said, "I have a wish which you can grant."

"Your wishes are my commands," Tristan answered humbly, looking at the floor.

"Tristan! You have the three gifts which I most value in a companion, for you are skilful at hunting, music and languages. I want you to be my squire and close companion. We will hunt by day; in the evenings we will talk with visitors from foreign lands who seek our hospitality and at night, when sleep comes slowly to our heavy heads, we will sing and play sweet music. If you will be my companion in these pastimes, Tristan, I will do my best for you with gold and horses and fine clothes."

"Sire, I am yours to command" said Tristan and he kissed the King's shoe.

"Then take charge of my sword and my bow and my gold-mounted horn, for from this moment you, Tristan, are the squire of my body."

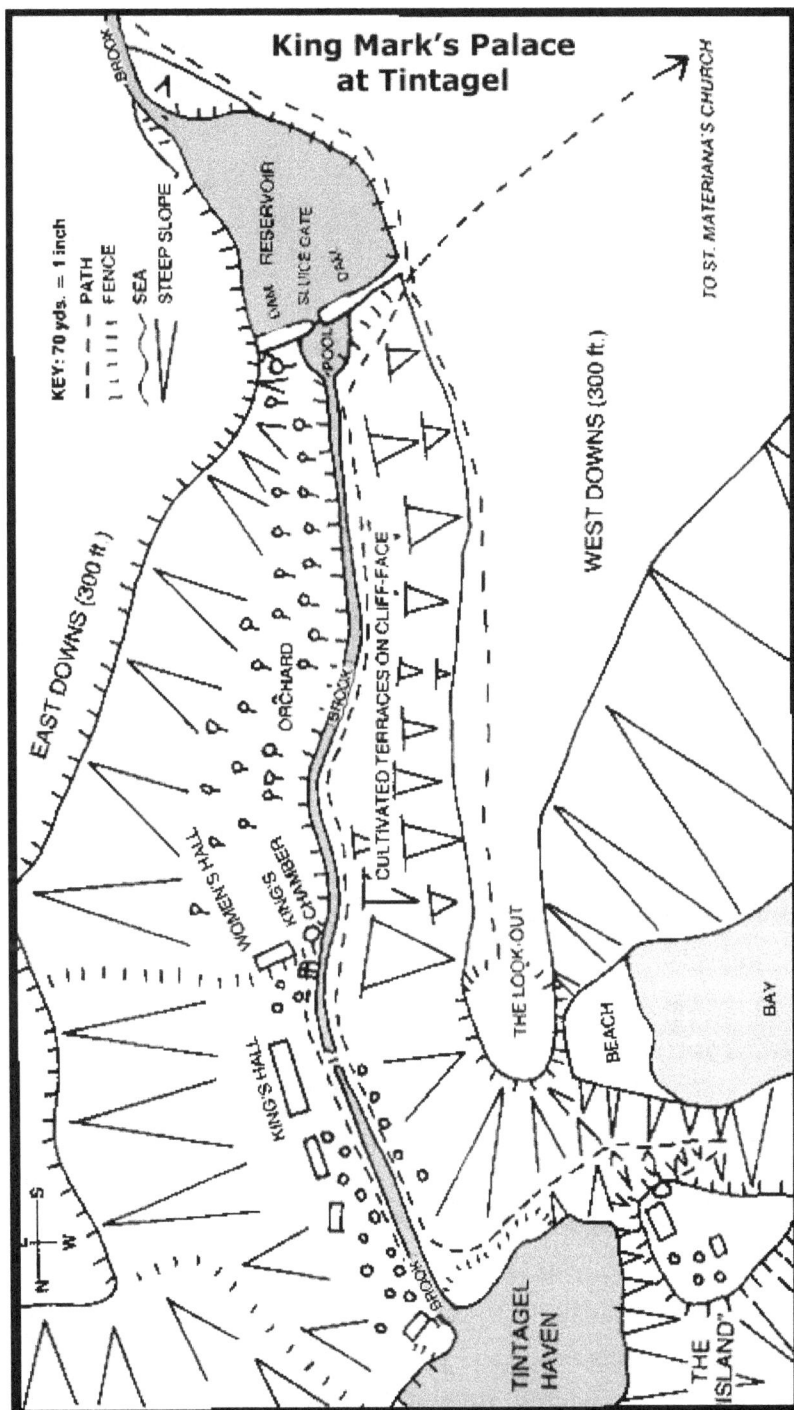

King Mark's Palace
at Tintagel

KEY: 70 yds. = 1 inch

- - - - PATH
٤٤٤٤٤ FENCE
〰〰〰 SEA
ﬧﬧﬧ STEEP SLOPE

RESERVOIR

DAM
SLUICE GATE
DAM
POOL

TO ST. MATERIANA'S CHURCH

BROOK

WEST DOWNS (300 ft.)

EAST DOWNS (300 ft.)

ORCHARD

BROOK

CULTIVATED TERRACES ON CLIFF-FACE

WOMEN'S HALL

KING'S
CHAMBER

KING'S HALL

THE LOOK-OUT

BEACH

BAY

N
S
W
E

BROOK

TINTAGEL
HAVEN

THE
"ISLAND"

CHAPTER 3

THE KING'S HEIR

For three years Tristan served King Mark as the squire of his body and he hardly ever left his master. He served the King at table, carving his meat and bread and tasting for poison everything that he ate or drank; he stood behind the King in his court; he rode next to the King on journeys and hunting; he sang and played, when the King was unwell or ill-tempered and he slept at the foot of the King's bed, from the time when he undressed him at night until he dressed him again in the morning. The King, who was afraid to give his trust and affection to any of his subjects, became more and more fond of the foundling, Tristan.

Tintagel became Tristan's home and he knew every building. The King's camp commanded the best landing-place in the sheltered haven, from which tin was shipped and it had been built in the narrow valley, because on the windy downs neither fruit nor grain could thrive nor man nor beast could keep warm in winter. The palace was protected both from the weather and from robbers by the high, steep sides of the valley and by the reservoir and dam at the valley's inland end, but the real stronghold of King Mark was built on "The Island" nearby.

The Island was not truly quite an island, since it was joined to the mainland by a narrow ridge of rock. That causeway could easily be defended and on the other sides of the Island, its cliffs dropped steeply into deep water. The King's stronghold was built on the leeward side of the Island, on a shelf of rock overlooking the causeway and the haven. There a cluster of stone beehive cells and a tiny chapel huddled within a stone wall. Although these buildings were within bowshot of the mainland, the wind around the Island was so strong and fitful that accurate shooting was impossible. King Mark's stronghold was very safe but very uncomfortable and he lived there only when serious danger threatened.

One morning, when the King returned from Mass, a courtier told Tristan that a beggar from Tristan's homeland had been asking for him. Tristan ran to the gate and found an old man talking to the porter. The old man wore only a single threadbare gown with neither shoes nor stockings and his hair and beard were rough-cut and tangled but he was very tall and strongly built.

Tristan shouted with joy: "Blessed, thrice blessed be the name of the Lord for allowing me to see you again, dear Father!"

Father and son rushed into each other's arms and kissed, weeping and laughing with emotion. Then Tristan asked, "How are my mother and my brothers, Father? Tell me their news."

"Indeed, I do not know how they are now, my son," Ronald answered. "For it is a long time since I saw them. When last I saw them, they were well except for their sorrow at losing you."

"You look both tired and ill-provided, Father. Have you fallen on poor times?"

"It was losing you, my son, that most impoverished me."

"Then I shall bring back your riches, Father. Come into the hall, so that I can present you to my lord, the King."

"I cannot enter a king's court dressed like this, my son," Ronald protested.

"Nonsense, Father! The King must see you first and after that you can change your clothes."

"Well!" Ronald muttered. "It is true that a man who brings good news is welcome whatever he wears. Therefore lead on, my son."

Tristan took Ronald by the hand and led him into the court and the courtiers stared in astonishment at the shabby old man with a weather-beaten face and unkempt hair.

"Who is this man?" King Mark asked sternly.

"He is my father, Lord King" Tristan answered. "He has sought for me in many lands and happily has now come to the end of his quest. If you would grant him your hospitality, Sire, I should very much like to have his company."

"Welcome, good master!" the King said to Ronald, and to Tristan he said, "Take our guest to the guest room; serve him with hot water and whatever else he needs to refresh him after his travels. Then give him clothing suited to his station and bring him to dine at my table."

When Ronald was bathed and dressed in fine clothes from the King's chests, Tristan led him back into the King's hall and the courtiers agreed that Tristan's father now looked like the rich merchant whom Tristan had described. Indeed, many of them said that Ronald looked more like a chieftain than a trader and they reminded one another how the huntsman had said that Tristan could not have learnt his woodmanship from a merchant.

The King had waited dinner until Tristan's father was ready. Now he seated his guest next to himself; they washed their hands and the trestle-tables were set up above their knees.

"Tristan!" said the King, "wait upon your father yourself.

"Tristan willingly served both the King and his father, and Ronald, his search now ended, ate well. But at last the tables were removed and stacked against the wall. Then the King asked his guest for news of his countrymen and Ronald answered, "Sire, it is three years since I left my country and, since I left it, I have been interested only in the quest which took me from home. Therefore,

Sire, I can give you no recent news of my countrymen. But, when I left them, they were as well as they could be, considering their sad loss."

"What was the loss which grieved your country, stranger? And what was your long quest?"

"To both questions one answer, Sire! Tristan here!"

"Tell your story, stranger," the King commanded.

"Sire, although the loss was very great and although the quest was long and hard, the story is quickly told. Tristan was stolen from me by rascally Norse traders and not only my family but the whole of Lothian mourned for my loss. Full of hope, I loaded a large chest of treasure into my ship and I sailed the seas to Norway and Denmark, to Frisia and Frankland, searching for Tristan. I visited many courts and questioned many travellers.

"After two years' travelling my treasure was exhausted and I sent my men home but I myself searched on through the wide world as a barefoot beggar. At last by God's grace I met two pilgrims, who were visiting holy places as penance for some sin and those good men told me of a boy whom they had once met, a boy who spoke Latin like a priest and who taught woodmanship to huntsmen.

"I asked the pilgrims what the boy looked like and, when they described his face, form and clothes, I asked them eagerly, 'Friends, do you know what happened to that boy?' They told me that they believed that he had become page to the King of Cornwall in Tintagel. Since that moment, Sire, I have rested neither night nor day, except when my legs could carry me no further."

King Mark sat thoughtfully for a while. Then he said, "Stranger, it puzzles me that a merchant should so neglect his family and business and that he should consume so much time and treasure to find a young lad. Ought you not rather to have stayed at home, to settle your other sons in trade and to find rich husbands for your daughters?"

Ronald sat quietly for a long time, but at last he looked King Mark straight in the eye and said, "Sire, if I dared, I could tell a story which would pierce your heart."

"Good stranger, while you are here, you need never fear to be injured for telling the truth," the King assured him. And the courtiers crowded around Ronald and begged, 'Tell us the whole story, good trader. Tell us why you searched so eagerly for Tristan."

"Sire," Ronald began. "I must tell you first that my trade is the noble trade of arms and that once upon a time I was the marshal and chief vassal of a young king. It happened that, when my young lord had cleared his lands of his enemies and had secured his boundaries against his neighbours, he went abroad to find adventure and left me as regent, to look after his kingdom in his absence.

"My lord took ship with a score of noblemen and reached another land and there he received generous hospitality. On a certain feast-day the king of that country held a great court and commanded his warriors and guests to show their strength and skill in games. My lord, so I have heard, was winner of the games and warlike trials and certainly, although he did not know it, he won that day the heart of the king's fair sister. For I must tell you that my lord was not only a brave warrior and a skilful athlete, he was also very good-looking.

"At the end of the games my lord greeted the lady with polite respect but she said sternly: 'If you put right the wrong which you have done me, I may call you honourable.'

"My puzzled lord asked what wrong he had done her but all she answered was: 'The reproach remains, until you have made amends.' And she sighed and said no more.

"From that day the princess was troubled by the pangs of love and my young lord was troubled by her reproachful words. But the more my lord thought about the reproach, the more his thoughts centered on the princess, until he was as much in love as she. The princess lived in the women's quarters of the palace, whereas my lord lived with the young warriors in the king's hall and it was difficult for the lovers to test each other's feelings. But day by day, by means of gestures, sighs and loving glances, each became more certain of the other's love and their yearning thoughts and unsettled hopes became a fiery passion, so that they were eager to meet alone.

"With great difficulty the lovers arranged a meeting but it was so short that they could only confirm that each loved the other more than life itself, and the very next day fate turned against them. A neighbouring king attacked that country and my lord took up arms, to help his host against the invader. I have heard that my lord did great deeds of valour in the battle but the invader was victorious and my lord himself was run through with a spear and carried back to his host's palace to die.

"Sire, I ask you to imagine the grief of that fair lady, the princess, for rumours of her lover's death continually reached the women's quarters and she herself nearly died both for pity of her lover's pain and for fear of never seeing him again. But her desperate need contrived a desperate plan and she begged her nurse, who never let her out of her sight, to arrange for her to visit the dying warrior, dressed as a healer. The old nurse pitied the lovelorn girl but also hoped for a reward. Furthermore, she considered that a man who had been spitted right through the belly from front to back must inevitably die, so that no harm could come of the escapade.

"The old nurse then paid a visit to the hut where my wounded lord lay dying and, while consoling him in his misfortune, she told him that the princess wished to visit him. The nurse returned to dress her mistress up as an old witch who was skilled in healing and my lord gave orders that the old witch should be admitted to his hut alone, so that she could work her magic undisturbed.

"So it happened that the lovers met in the most pitiful way, for my lord was wounded to death and in great pain and the noble princess was distracted with grief. She sat beside his bed; they looked deeply into each other's eyes and their eyes spoke more of love than if they had spent the whole day talking. Then the lady kissed my lord's pale face on the forehead, the eyes, the cheeks, the lips and, having reached his lips, she could not stop kissing him. She slipped from her seat and gathered in her arms his nearly lifeless body and, by pressing her heart against his heart, she tried to give her life to him.

"Then, Sire, God performed a miracle, for the princess did put life into my dying lord. The fire of love lit a small flame in his carcase. His pale lips kissed her and his feeble arms embraced her. The small flame flared brightly for a while and love flew like lightning from one to the other. Yes, Sire! The golden delights of love embroidered for a while the black raiment of pain and death.

"Strange to say, from that day my lord began to mend and after a few months he was able to walk. My lord and his lady, the princess, contrived to meet sometimes. They thought of nothing but each other and would have been content to go on like that forever. But again fate turned against them, for messengers arrived to warn my lord that his ancient enemy had invaded his lands.

"I ask you to imagine, Lord King, the grief in their hearts and the tears in their eyes, when my lord came to say goodbye to his lady, the princess.

" 'How I suffer for your sake!' the princess cried. 'For I carry three burdens, each of which is enough to crush me. First, I carry your child and, unless God helps me, I cannot survive his birth. Second, when my brother hears of my wrongdoing, he will kill me shamefully. Third, even if my brother does not kill me, he will disinherit me. Then I shall be poor and my child will be poor and both his life and mine will be made miserable by the disgrace which we have brought upon my family and people. Alas! I shall never again be happy,' she wailed. Then my lord comforted her and dried her eyes. 'I did not know that you were with child, dear love,' he said. 'And I shall not desert you, for you have saved my life and made me very happy. Either I shall stay here with you, to face your brother, or else you shall come home with me'

"At once the princess took heart and said firmly: 'We cannot stay here in freedom and contentment. My brother will be furious, when he hears of the dishonour which we have brought upon him. Even if he does not kill both you and me, he is sure to kill our son rather than have a bastard in the family. It will be best if I slip quietly away and join your ship just before you sail'.

"When my lord's ship was ready to sail, he went boldly ashore to take leave of the king, and the princess went secretly aboard with all her jewels and a few clothes. Then, the moment that my lord returned aboard, the ship cast off. The lovers put to sea on the evening tide and they were far away in the friendly dark, before the king heard that his sister had eloped.

"My lord and his lady were welcomed with honour by the people of Lothian and they were married in the sight of all the great men of the realm. But for a third time, fate turned against the dear lovers. In battle against the English invaders, my lord the King was killed, and my lady his Queen was so cast down by grief that she never spoke another word. But in her mortal anguish she gave birth to a little son."

Ronald wiped his eye with the back of his hand. "Sire!" he said. "Both the King and the Queen, my dear lord and lady, died in one day and they left us only a tiny scrap of their flesh and blood, a baby boy. That baby could do nothing against King Morgan and the Northumbrians and we, the defeated men of Lothian, had to make what terms we could. We made peace with Morgan and swore ourselves his men."

"But what happened to the baby boy, the rightful heir to his father's kingdom?" asked King Mark.

"For fear of King Morgan" Ronald replied quietly, "I declared that my young king had died in his mother's belly and I gave the child to my wife and told her to pretend that the child was our own."

Ronald sat for a long time, looking at his feet. Then he raised his head and looked first at Tristan and then at King Mark. "That baby boy was Tristan," he said. "I named him Tristan, because he was conceived and born in sorrow. Tristan's father was King Tulloch of Lothian, who twenty years ago fought to defend Cornwall against its enemies and Tristan's mother was that gracious and lovely lady, the Princess Whiteflower, your own sister, most noble King.

"Tristan is not my son," Ronald declared. "He is my lord and I am his faithful vassal. In order to educate my lord as befits a king, I have spent my treasure and, in order to save him from slavery, I have worn out my life in travel."

"That is a strange story," King Mark said thoughtfully. "And I confess that I almost believe it without any proof at all. But tell me, noble Marshall, how can I be sure that this boy is my sister's child?"

Ronald pushed his finger into a wallet which he carried under his robes, threaded on the girdle of his drawers. "Tristan's mother wore this ring, Sire," he said and held up a gold ring set with a pink stone.

"My father's ring," cried King Mark, "which I gave my sister as a token of my love!"

"Come, kiss me, Tristan. Let me congratulate you," King Mark called but Tristan looked sullen and sad.

"I have no reason to join in the general merriment," he grumbled. "For the dear father whom I have just found after being orphaned for three long years has now renounced me, and the noble father of whom I have heard for the very first time is as dead as a doornail. So I have been bereaved twice in one day."

Ronald reproved him. "You have little cause for complaint, Tristan. For today you have learnt that you are a king's heir, with an ancient kingdom for your inheritance. Furthermore, I am still your loving foster-father and I am still both your marshal and your most faithful vassal."

Then suddenly King Mark cried out: "Ah! Now I remember how young King Tulloch used to praise the man who, he said, was his friend and counsellor, his right-hand man and strong support. 'Faithful Ronald' he called that fine man. Tell me, Tristan. Is this noble chieftain, your foster-father Ronald, surnamed 'the faithful'?"

"Sire, it is so," Tristan answered. "As you have just heard, there was never a man more truly named, for never did any vassal serve his lord better and more unselfishly than Faithful Ronald has served my father and me."

Ronald received his due of praise from everyone, and King Mark himself rose from his seat and kissed him on both cheeks as a token of his respect.

But, when the Cornishmen had shown Ronald their admiration, King Mark said to Tristan in the hearing of all who were in his long hall, "Listen carefully, Tristan. I shall prove to you that not only have you <u>not</u> lost two fathers in one day but you have really <u>gained</u> two fathers. You have on the one hand found your fosterer, Faithful Marshal Ronald, and he loves you now no less than he did when you believed him to be your father in the blood. You have on the other hand, found a second father; I am your uncle, your nearest surviving male kinsman and I am glad to undertake the - duties of father which our customs impose on an orphan's next of kin. Therefore rejoice, my son, for today you have found two fathers."

Then for the first time King Mark gave Tristan the three kisses on the cheeks which were the recognised acknowledgment of kinship. When he had kissed Tristan in the sight of all, he announced in the hearing of all: "Tristan, not only have you become my son by adoption, you are also my next of kin and my heir presumptive. That is to say that, unless I marry and have children by my lawful wife, you will inherit my lands and sovereignty."

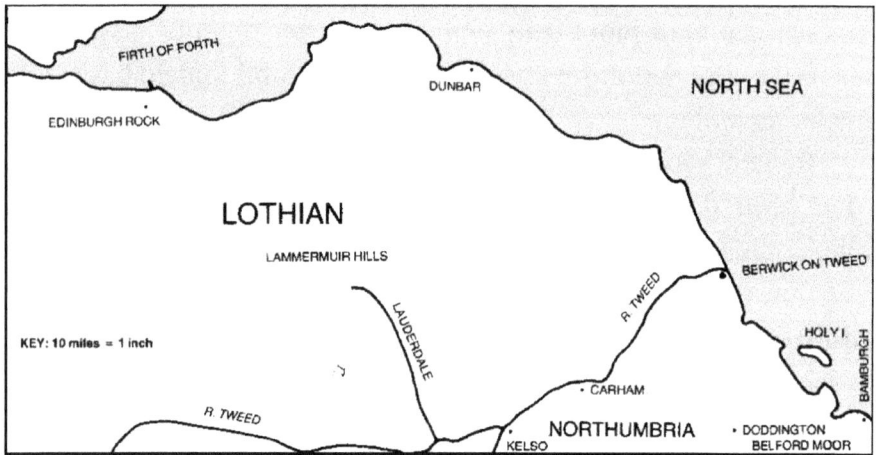

CHAPTER 4

THE AVENGER

"By my advice," Faithful Marshal Ronald said to Tristan, "you should quickly ask your two foster-fathers to help you to regain your father's inheritance, for you are nineteen years old and of age to bear arms and to rule a kingdom. King Mark knows that you have been well taught and that you are worthy to be a warrior. Ask him to grant you arms and to give you ships and warriors. If you are willing to try your luck against King Morgan of Northumbria, I will undertake to bring the chiefs and warriors of Lothian to your aid, and I will support you with both my power and my advice."

"You need not be shy to ask my help, Tristan," King Mark assured him. "You can count on my treasure and my war-host, if you need them."

"Sire!" Tristan addressed the King. "First of all, I seek the honour of receiving my arms from your hands, for there is no king in all the world from whom I would rather have them. But, when I am a warrior, my first duty will be to avenge the death of my father and the theft of my lands and for that purpose I shall ask you, my new father, to aid me with warriors and treasure."

"My son!" said the King. "Consult with your fosterer and faithful friend, the good Marshal here. Choose thirty young noblemen as your companions in arms and make ready whatever men and ships you need, for I undertake to meet all the expenses of your expedition. Meanwhile, I shall seek out arms and armour which it will be an honour both for me to give and for you to receive."

King Mark sent trusted men with a shipload of tin to the River Rhine, for the Frankish iron-workers of the Rhineland made the strongest and lightest body armour of iron mail and helmets of welded iron plates and they also made the hardest and sharpest weapons in Europe. After the winter King Mark's purveyors brought back mail byrnies, helmets, spear-blades and swords for thirty warriors. Long, straight poles of ash and straight-grained planks of seasoned lime-wood were selected for the spear-shafts and shields of Tristan and his men. The spear-shafts were forced into the sockets of the iron blades; the planks were riveted together and covered with oxhide, to make round shields and the rims and hand-holds of the shields were protected with iron.

For Tristan himself, King Mark chose the best arms and armour. Every single link of Tristan's mail byrnie and his iron helmet, both inside and out, were plated with tin, to keep them free from rust. A gilded boar's head crest was cast by an expert for the top of his war-hat and his wooden shield was faced with a sheet of copper and decorated with a boar's head device in black leather. His spear-head was bound onto its shaft with blue and red beads strung on copper wire, and his sword-hilt and scabbard-mountings were gilded and decorated with red and blue enamel. With Ronald's help Tristan had trained thirty young noblemen to be his companions and armoured warriors. He chose one hundred hunters who were skilful with both the bow and the sling, to be his light spearmen. After Easter he hired three Frisian ships with their captains and seamen, and by Whitsun his expedition was ready. On Whitsun Eve Tristan and his thirty noble companions were stripped naked by their friends and ducked in the sea to wash away all impurities and they were dressed in new trousers and tunics of white linen, and new cloaks of red and blue wool. Then they were led to the little church on the downs nearby and left there all night to pray beside their arms.

The young men heard the first mass of Whit Sunday and carried their arms to King Mark's hall. Tristan was led to the King's high seat and the King struck him on the shoulder with the flat of his sword, saying, "My son Tristan, after this one blow from me never accept a blow from any other man without immediately returning it. That is a warrior's duty. Be kind to the poor, be proud to the rich and be generous and loyal to all who deserve it."

Then the King asked Ronald to help him equip Tristan in his bright byrnie and crested helmet, his shield, spear and sword and, when Tristan was armed, Ronald cried, "May God in Heaven grant you good luck, my own dear lord!"

Tristan turned proudly in his shining armour to make warriors of his companions. One by one, he buffeted each of the thirty young men and told him never to let any other man strike him without immediately taking vengeance. The Cornish chiefs helped Tristan to arm his companions and at last the companions stood around their chief, as powerful a warrior-band as could be found in Europe at that time. Mail shirts and the hard, patterned swords of the Rhineland were still a costly rarity and it was not often that a chieftain had his own band of thirty warriors so well equipped.

The rest of that day was consumed in war-games and sports and feasting, but the next morning Tristan, Faithful Ronald, his thirty young warriors, and his one hundred young spearmen took leave of their friends.

King Mark's last words to Tristan were: "Tristan, I shall miss you sorely and I hope that, when you have won your kingdom, you will return to me, for you are my dearly loved son and after my death

Cornwall will be yours. Meanwhile, listen carefully to the advice of your faithful marshal and be generous and loyal to your thirty companions, so that they will serve you gladly. May God and His Son watch over you! And remember that your prosperity and your honour now depend on you. Guard them well."

Tristan and his men made a quick voyage to Edinburgh and Ronald soon persuaded the chiefs of Lothian to bend the knee to Tristan as their rightful King. Once again the ancient kingdom stirred eagerly and everywhere men took their arms from their hiding-places, and swore to be revenged on the hated English who had been their masters for nearly twenty years.

Tristan, however, stayed in Edinburgh only long enough to take the loyal oaths of all his father's vassals. He mustered his thirty sworn companions and his one hundred spearmen and early one morning, he rode out on the road to Bamburgh, where King Morgan, the King of Northumbria, lived on a fortified rock. On the first night out Tristan slept in the Lammermuir Hills in the south of Lothian and the next day he hurried down the old coast road over the River Tweed and past Holy Island. On the third day, Tristan halted on Belford Moor and he left his spearmen there to build a stockade on the high ground. But Tristan and his thirty companions covered their helmets, byrnies and swords with woollen cowls and plaids, and took fresh horses. Then they cantered on to Bamburgh.

Supper was nearly finished in King Morgan's hall and the ale-jugs were going round quickly. Suddenly an usher ran into announce: "A party of strangers has arrived, Lord King. Their chief is a handsome youth who says that he has urgent business with you."

"Stack their spears outside the porch and bring the men in" the King commanded.

When Tristan and his youthful friends were led into the King's high hall, the burly English warriors sitting behind the long side tables looked at them with scorn but Tristan marched straight towards the King, who sat on the dais at the far end of the hall. King Morgan had been ruling a troublesome kingdom for more than twenty years and he was a proud old fighter. He relied on no-one else to protect him from this beardless stripling but he held his sword between his knees and allowed Tristan to walk right up to the step of the dais. Tristan bent the knee and bared his head respectfully.

"Lord King, may God bless you in accordance with the way that you treat me!" he greeted King Morgan. "I have come to you, because I am of full age to rule the lands which I ought to hold by rightful inheritance from my father. I require you to account for the revenues which you have taken from my lands during my childhood and I require you to grant me possession of my lands immediately. In return I will give you such service as a freeman may honourably give his lord."

"Who are you? And who were your parents?" King Morgan asked.

"My name is Tristan. My father was King Tulloch of Lothian and my mother was Queen Whiteflower, the sister of the noble King Mark of Cornwall."

"You are a good-looking boy, Tristan and, if your claim was good, I should not dispute it. But I never heard that Tulloch had a lawful heir." Casually King Morgan added: "I heard that Tulloch had a love affair with a Cornish girl and carried her off against her brother's will but I never heard that he had a son born in wedlock."

"Are you calling me a bastard?" Tristan demanded angrily.

"It was you and not I who spoke the vile word but, unless I have proof to the contrary Tristan, that is how it seems to me."

Lord God, is it not enough that this man killed my father and my mother, without him calling me a bastard? Tristan thought, but aloud he said, "King Morgan, I ask you two questions. Would the King of Cornwall have acknowledged me his son by adoption and his heir by blood, if he thought me a bastard? Would Marshal Ronald and all the chiefs of Lothian have laid their hands in mine and acknowledged me their lord, if they thought me a bastard?"

"I need PROOF," King Morgan said doggedly. "And neither your claims nor the bad breath of the slavish riff-raff of Cornwall and Lothian mean anything to me. Your father broke his oath, when he rebelled against my father and I have taken back what belonged to me by right of inheritance, the sovereignty of Lothian. What I have I hold and I hold it by force," King Morgan shouted. "Yes! Against the twittering complaints of a cock-sparrow like you my defence is this."

As King Morgan spoke, he kicked the kneeling boy full in the mouth. Tristan tasted blood and he saw red. With one movement he leapt to his feet, drew his sword from his plaid and brought it down back-handed on King Morgan's head. King Morgan was wearing only a little leather cap and he crashed to the floor with his head split open. "There is my title-deed," Tristan yelled, and he thrust his sword through the corpse.

As the quarrel on the dais had sharpened, both Tristan's thirty men and the English warriors who sat around the hall felt for their weapons. Then suddenly, the terrible deed was done and pandemonium broke out. Tristan's men attacked at once, before the Englishmen could get out from behind their heavy tables. The Cornish were outnumbered three to one but they had been expecting a desperate battle and they were wearing helmets and mail shirts beneath their clothes. The Englishmen, on the other hand, were full of food and drink; they wore no armour and, though they jumped up to avenge their lord, they had no leader.

While along the side walls the battle hung in doubt, Tristan defended himself against the King's squires who leapt at him from the dais. Step by step he retreated down the hall. Then suddenly he sounded a blast on his horn. His men turned and ran out into the yard and, while they were getting their spears and mounting their horses, Tristan felled every Englishman who tried to follow. Finally he himself ducked out of the hall and leapt onto his horse.

The guards at the gate were armed and alert but Tristan and his men cut their way out of the powerful fort and galloped away.

The sun had set but the midsummer evening is long, and by the time that Tristan and his companions had reached the foot of Belford Moor, they were outnumbered and hard pressed. But Tristan's horn summoned the men whom he had left building a camp on the moor and a hundred Cornish spearmen poured down the hillside in the gathering dusk. For a moment, the English fell back in surprise and alarm, and Tristan and his men were able to retreat into their stockade.

During the night the English of Northumbria gathered from every side, eager to avenge their murdered lord. King Morgan's brother took command and he swore by all the gods whom he could think of, neither to take off his mail byrnie nor to lay his head on a pillow until Tristan was dead. He surrounded Tristan's stockade to prevent his escape and at dawn he attacked with overwhelming force.

Tristan, however, had planned his campaign very carefully with Faithful Ronald. As soon as he had entered the stockade at nightfall, he had ordered his weary companions and their squires to ride out at the rear. With them went all the horses except those which were wounded or utterly spent. In spite of the noise which the horses made, that advance party got away unnoticed, before the English had blockaded the rear of Tristan's camp. During the night his lightly armed spearmen, experienced hunters all, slipped away westwards by twos and threes. Those who remained within the stockade made a show of strength by loosing arrows and slinging stones towards the camp fires of the English. They shouted and provoked the horses to neigh and squeal, so that the English supposed that the whole of Tristan's band was still in the camp.

When at dawn the Northumbrian host ran up the hill to storm the stockade, they met no resistance and they found only a few badly wounded men and some hamstrung horses. Tristan and his footmen had crept away under cover of the night, to join their companions with the horses on the Roman road near Doddington, and by the time that the English had mounted their horses and started in pursuit, Tristan's force was riding as fast as wounds and weariness would allow towards Carham on Tweed. Tristan's small party had to fight desperately before they reached the marshy valley of the Tweed, but hidden in the marsh and veiled by the dusk, they at last found safety.

In the morning, the Northumbrian host divided in two. The main body marched up the right bank of the Tweed to cross the river at Kelso, where an English burgh guarded the ford and the rest hunted Tristan's band among the marshes. Either on one river-bank or on the other the English felt sure of catching their enemy; but Tristan had laid a trap for them.

Marshal Ronald had mustered the full host of Lothian in Lauderdale, and when the English had crossed the river and started down the left bank to cut off Tristan, the host of Lothian came roaring down upon their left flank and hemmed them in against the river. Tristan and his men had also crossed the river during the night, for a fleet of skin-boats had been hidden at Carham to help him in his retreat, and now the well-armed Cornish companions thrust into the battle like an iron wedge, driving towards the banner of the Northumbrian King. Soon Morgan's brother had fulfilled his oath, but not in the way that he intended, for Tristan killed him, before ever he unarmed or put his head on a pillow and the English host was routed.

That day seemed long to the Englishmen, who were pursued until darkness hid them. Not many returned safely to Bamburgh.

Both in the battle and in the chase, Tristan fought like a tireless hero and during the next two days, he captured every English stronghold north of the Tweed. Then came the counting of the spoil and the burying of the dead, and it was not until three days after the battle that the host of Lothian, victorious but spent, returned to Edinburgh to celebrate their victory.

Tristan had sent messengers ahead of his return, to bid his foster-mother, Ronald's wife, to prepare a lavish feast. Tristan's sworn companions and the chiefs of Lothian feasted and made merry, until at last, on the third day of the feast, Tristan called for silence. With formal ceremony he made Ronald's sons companions of his band, binding them to him with oaths of personal service. Then he spoke to the great assembly: "By the help of God and of all you who are gathered here, I have avenged my father and proved my title to the Kingdom of Lothian and my title is the same as that by which King Morgan held it— the strength of my hand.

"My grandfather held Lothian as a vassal of the King of Northumbria but my father Tulloch won the full sovereignty by defeating the English in battle and now I have confirmed that sovereignty and established my frontier on the River Tweed.

"Nevertheless, I intend to return to Cornwall, in order to serve the good King Mark who granted me my arms. And so I must give Lothian a guardian and ruler. Here in your presence I grant all the honours and all the revenues which I derive from my Kingdom of Lothian to Faithful Ronald and his heirs for ever. Long live King Ronald of Lothian."

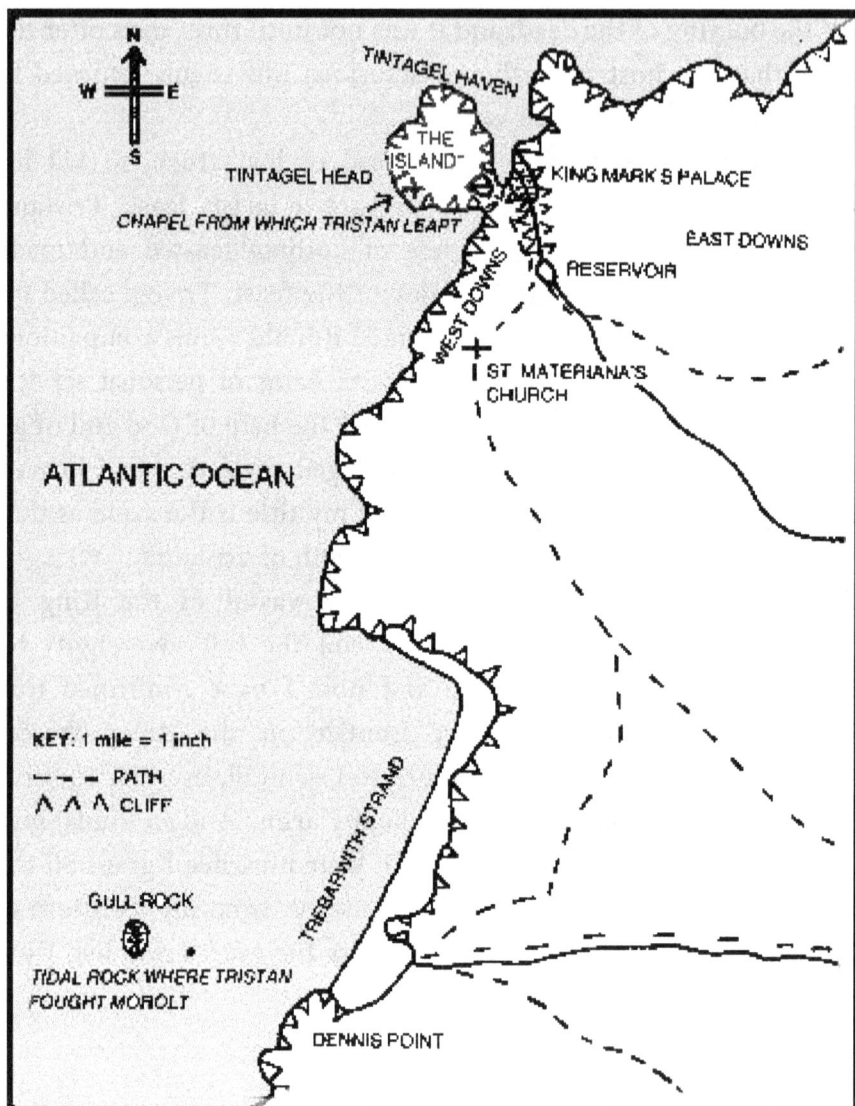

N

W ──┼── E

S

TINTAGEL HAVEN

THE "ISLAND"

TINTAGEL HEAD

KING MARK'S PALACE

CHAPEL FROM WHICH TRISTAN LEAPT

EAST DOWNS

WEST DOWNS

RESERVOIR

ST MATERIANA'S CHURCH

ATLANTIC OCEAN

KEY: 1 mile = 1 inch

─ ─ ─ PATH

∧ ∧ ∧ CLIFF

TREBARWITH STRAND

GULL ROCK

TIDAL ROCK WHERE TRISTAN FOUGHT MOROLT

DENNIS POINT

CHAPTER 5

THE DEFENDER

When the people of Lothian heard that Tristan intended to leave them and to return to Cornwall, they were sad and sorry for although he had been their leader for only a few days, he was already their hero— well-born, handsome, brave and, they thought, lucky. The saddest and sorriest of them all was Faithful Ronald. Although he had gained the Kingdom of Lothian by Tristan's decision, he truly loved his foster-son and he would rather have had Tristan's company than his kingdom. Nevertheless, Ronald faithfully obeyed his lord in this matter as in everything else. So he escorted Tristan aboard his ship with all the honour due to an emperor. For farewell gifts, he gave him the master who had previously been his tutor and a magnificent Irish wolfhound called Huden.

The tears flowed in Lothian when Tristan sailed away but he looked forward to an enthusiastic welcome from King Mark and the people of Cornwall. In order to shorten the sea journey, he landed at Fowey on the south coast of Cornwall and rode with his companions across the country towards Tintagel. Long before they reached Tintagel, they had noticed the gloomy faces of the Cornishmen whom they passed and, when they asked for news, there was only one piece of news on everyone's lips. "The Irish ambassador has come for the tribute."

Tristan remembered that the Cornish had to pay a tribute to the Irish. Long ago, at that time when his father, Tullock, had been so badly wounded in King Mark's service, the Irish of Leinster had defeated the Cornishmen and the chiefs of Cornwall had bought their safety by promising to pay tribute every year. The tribute had been paid three times, while Tristan was a squire at King Mark's court. "I do not remember that there was much difficulty over collecting the tribute in previous years," Tristan said to his companions. "Why is it causing such distress this time?"

"You do not know the terms of the tribute, Sire," said one of his companions. "The first year's tribute is only three hundred copper pence; the second year's tribute is three hundred silver pence and the third year's tribute is three hundred pennyweight of gold. But the fourth year we must send thirty noble boys. Last year it was gold; so this year it is boys. Next year, if God lets us live so long in our shame, it will be copper again."

"Shameful indeed!" exclaimed Tristan. "But let us hurry to Tintagel, to see what is happening!"

Tristan had expected to be received at Tintagel with joy and honour, but the King's hall resounded with agonised weeping and desperate prayers and the King himself was too grief-stricken even to welcome Tristan. Every chieftain in Cornwall had been summoned to appear at Tintagel with all his boy-children between the ages of seven and eleven. They were waiting for the drawing of lots to decide which children must be given to the Irish. Fathers were praying to their favourite saints to save their children in the fateful lottery; mothers were cursing their men for submitting to so barbarous a tribute and lamenting the day that they had borne boys fated to become slaves, and the children themselves were crying aloud in fear. It was a pitiful sight and King Mark wept, as he sat on his dais to supervise the drawing of lots.

Tristan was vexed because his uncle had not welcomed him and he was disgusted to see the Cornish chiefs so feeble-hearted. With loud scorn he asked King Mark: "Is it true, Sire, that the noblemen of Cornwall have offered their children to be the slaves of Irishmen across the sea?"

"Thirty well-born and well-brought-up boys must go to Leinster as this year's tribute. That is the truth, my son," King Mark answered sadly.

"By what right do these men send into slavery children who were born not only free, but noble?"

"The Irish ambassador demands it, Tristan."

"By what title does an Irishman demand that Cornish chieftains[7] sons should be enslaved to serve Irishmen?"

"It has been the custom ever since the Irish defeated my war-host twenty one years ago. We must pay the tribute, unless we are willing to fight the Irish."

"Then let Cornwall prepare for war, Sire! Here before me sits the richest and the most courageous king in Christendom. Here behind me I have my warrior-band, fresh from conquering another oppressor. Here around me stand the Cornish nobles, strong, well-made men, burning, I believe, to wreak revenge on their Irish tyrants. Lead us into battle, Sire." cried Tristan. "Tell the Irish ambassador that, if his king wants anything from us, we will pay him with spears and swords."

"I have sometimes thought that we could now defeat the Irish, if it came to war," King Mark said. "But by the terms of our treaty the Irish have a choice. They can choose to fight either host against host or in a single combat, the Irish champion against the Cornish champion."

"Better still, Sire, to throw off the tribute without the expense and losses of a war! Command your noble chiefs to select with care the strongest, bravest and most experienced warrior among them. If the Irish choose to decide the matter by single combat, let that honoured man be ready to fight for Cornwall's right."

"Nephew, you do not understand how the matter stands," King Mark said crossly. "The ambassador who has come for the tribute of boys is himself the Irish champion and it is certain that he will choose to settle the matter by a single combat."

"Better, Sire, and better!" cried Tristan. "For the matter can be quickly settled. By the grace of God and through the valour of your noble champion Cornwall will be free again tonight."

But King Mark said sadly, "Tristan, you have not <u>seen</u> the Irish champion, the mighty Norseman Morolt. I have begged my chiefs to find me a champion to fight this Viking giant but no-one will face him."

Then Tristan turned and cried down the hall: "Chieftains and noblemen, warriors and friends, I beg you to tell me that my uncle is mistaken. Surely every man of you is willing to fight to save his family? Surely every man here would rather lose his life than see his children sold into slavery?"

But the Cornishmen looked glum and they made no answer. Therefore, Tristan tried to encourage them: "My friends, I implore you, since right is on your side, put away such shameful fear. Agree among yourselves, my noble lords, that the best fighter of you all will stand ready to face Morolt if he chooses to enforce the tribute by a single combat and undertake that the rest of you will bow your heads and bend your knees in prayer, calling on God to defend the righteous cause."

Still the Cornish chiefs hung their heads in shame and silence and their wives and sons filled the hall with their angry abuse and desperate disappointment.

Then Tristan told the King: "If none of these men will fight a combat in order to save his sons, I myself will do so, Lord King, in order to save your good name, for this tribute, Sire, is a disgrace to your own honour. I know that Morolt is a man of might and a brave, skilful and experienced warrior, whereas I am not yet grown to my full strength and my skill and experience are as yet small. Nevertheless, God defends the righteous and I believe that the Cornish cause is just. Such a tribute as I have heard described, is barbarous and beyond reason."

"Nephew!" said King Mark without enthusiasm, "you have not seen Morolt. When you see him, you will realise that the Cornish chiefs are not such silly cowards as you think, for no ordinary man can hope to escape death in a mortal combat against Morolt, even though Morolt is a pagan."

"How can you say that, Uncle? Brute force has often been humbled by righteous weakness, and it is with the help of my just cause and with the power of God Himself that I hope and trust to overcome Morolt, the heathen oppressor."

"I cannot allow you to throw away your life so foolishly, Tristan, for you are my companion and my only heir, " King Mark said firmly. But below the dais, in the body of the hall, new hope had silenced the wailing and had dried the tears.

"Good Tristan! Sire!" cried the Cornish chiefs and their families. "If you can win our freedom, we will love you for ever and honour you next after our king."

"Certainly, with God's help, I hope to win your freedom," Tristan assured them. "But first let us hear what Morolt has to say! For perhaps he will let the tribute go, when he hears that we mean to dispute it. Or, if he wishes to apply the test of arms, he may prefer to fight a full-scale war rather than a single combat."

When Morolt was summoned to the King's hall, Tristan saw that he was indeed a fearsome man, for he was seven foot tall and nearly covered in coarse red hair and his hands and feet were twice the size of Tristan's. Morolt supposed that the lots had been drawn and that the tribute was ready for him to take. He began to look around, for he wished to inspect the boys, in order to make sure that they all had the white skin of noblemen and that they were sound in wind and limb. But from the King's side Tristan asked Morolt, "What brings you to Cornwall, stranger?"

Morolt was surprised and he tugged at his beard, as he answered irritably: "You know quite well that I have come for the yearly tribute."

"By what title, stranger, do you demand tribute?"

"By the title of force, boy!" Morolt answered proudly.

"What is taken by force is taken by robbery and God knows that all good men ought to resist a robber. Therefore, from now on your force will be met with force, and we will have no more robbery of our treasure and our children. Indeed, we may soon decide to come to Ireland for the goods and children stolen from us these past twenty years. Go and tell your king that we will no longer pay tribute to him and tell him that, unless he sends back what he has wrongly taken, we shall come and get it."

Morolt was astonished to hear such words from the cowardly Cornish who had meekly paid tribute for so long and he asked King Mark, "Does this young cockerel speak with your approval, Lord King?"

"The Lord Tristan has my approval," King Mark answered. "Tell the King of Leinster that we will pay him no more tribute and that we demand the return of all that he has taken from us."

"We agree. We agree," shouted the Cornish chiefs.

"You are not only foolish but false and faithless, for the tribute is ours by right of a sworn treaty," Morolt shouted furiously. His blue eyes blazed and his red hair and beard bristled about his red face like the sparks about a brandished torch.

"Not so, Lord Ambassador! It is not so," Tristan replied calmly. "Under the treaty we have the right to dispute by arms the taking of the tribute and we do so dispute it. You, Sir Ambassador, must make up your mind. Either your war-host must prepare for battle; or else your champion must arm for single combat. The choice between these two types of combat is yours under the treaty."

"I have no war-host with me, as you very well know," muttered Morolt.

"He who comes to rob his neighbour should bring enough force to subdue him," Tristan pointed out. "But, if you are unprepared for battle, stranger, run away home to Ireland and give our message to your king. We will await his war-host; or else, by God, unless it arrives soon, we may come to Ireland to find it."

"Not so fast, cockerel! Not so fast! I have the choice of two types of combat and, even if I have not brought a war-host to enforce the tribute, I have a champion here who can conquer any Cornishman yet born."

Morolt challenged them with his eyes and thumped his chest. "When the morning tide begins to ebb," he said, "I shall row out alone to the tidal rocks off Trebarwith Strand, where my ships are beached. Send your champion to fight me there. Then you will see my title to the Cornish tribute, for this is it," he roared and waved aloft a hairy red fist as large as a leg of lamb.

"And this feeble hand" Tristan replied, "with God's help will prove the tribute to be robbery and no longer tolerable."

In the sight of all, the two champions shook hands on the undertaking to meet on the flat rocks opposite Dennis Point as soon as the tide had receded from them.

Morolt strode from the King's hall and rode over the downs towards his ships on Trebarwith Strand. After a good night's sleep, Tristan called for his arms. He threw off his red cloak and his embroidered tunic and he dressed himself in a knee-length tunic of

49

thick red cloth and a short-sleeved byrnie of interlinked mail. Then his squires braided his straggling young beard and his long brown hair into a dozen plaits, which stood out around his head like the spokes of a wheel around its hub; they loaded his forearms with broad bronze bracelets and they bound his trousers around his shins with red leather straps. One of his companions put his crested helmet on his head and tucked all his hair up under its iron rim. Another companion brought his round shield of wooden planks, which was faced with a sheet of beaten copper and emblazoned with a black boar's head. A third friend brought a nine foot spear and the King himself hung his gilded sword on his chest and kissed him three times, before he mounted his pony.

Tristan, escorted by his sworn companions and followed by the King and a crowd of desperate boys, went down to Trebarwith. A tent stood on the shore near the Irish ships which had come to carry the tribute of slaves, and outside the tent, exercising his muscles by striking with his sword at a baulk of timber stuck upright in the sand, was Morolt. He was dressed and armed in the same way as Tristan but the sword in his hand was longer than Tristan's; the shield which was slung from his neck was larger than Tristan's and hung on a shoulder-harness he carried an extra weapon, an axe with a "bearded" blade.

Tristan and his party dismounted on the sand opposite Gull Rock, which was so called because only gulls could surmount its cliffs. Between Gull Rock and the cliffs of Dennis Point swirling brown patches in the sea showed the position of the rocks where the combat was to be fought but it was a while before the ebbing tide had uncovered the flat rocks.

"Ahoy there!" Morolt shouted. "Now is the time to start our little game." And he waded into the sea and climbed into a small skin-boat, which one of his men was holding ready. Tristan did not at once follow Morolt's lead. He was gazing over the sea at the rock which would be the field of battle. It appeared to be covered with seaweed and slime. Suddenly he bent down and pulled off his leather shoes.

"You will cut your feet on the sharp shells," Master warned him.

"Better to cut my feet than to slip on wet leather and cut my head on Morolt's sword," Tristan answered seriously.

Before he rowed his coracle towards the rocks, he knelt in front of King Mark and asked both the King and all the people of Cornwall to pray for God's blessing on the Cornish cause. Morolt had landed on the largest rock and had pulled his boat up after him. But when Tristan jumped ashore, he pushed his boat away with his spear.

"Why have you turned your boat adrift?" Morolt asked in surprise.

Tristan looked around him and answered seriously, "I see only two men on this island and I am quite sure that not more than one will leave it. Therefore, one boat will be enough."

Morolt looked at Tristan with a new respect. "I like you, young man and I do not want to have to kill you. Confirm my right to the tribute and we can forget about the proposed fight."

"I should prefer peace;" said Tristan, "but only if the tribute is abolished."

"No! That is impossible," Morolt said firmly.

"Then let us talk no longer!" cried Tristan, who wanted the greatest advantage from his bare feet, while the rock and seaweed were still wet and slippery. "Since you are so confident of your ability to kill me, defend yourself, for I am coming for you."

Tristan drew back his spear at arm's length behind his shoulder and hurled it at Morolt, without letting go of it. But Morolt was the survivor of many hundreds of fights and Tristan's sudden attack did not catch him unawares. Almost carelessly, he moved his shield one way and his head the other. Tristan's spear-point went harmlessly past his ear and he replied with a jab which Tristan only just blocked with his shield.

For a long time the two champions hurled and thrust with their spears, and blocked and deflected with their shields but their byrnies stopped the few blows which their shields let pass. Only their arms were scratched and bleeding where their bracelets had not protected them. Neither man was seriously hurt but Tristan was the more tired. Morolt was hardly sweating and he was smiling calmly, for he had taken the battle very easily and had allowed Tristan to do all the attacking.

Tristan had been rushing Morolt, in the hope of making him slip but Morolt had been so little bothered by all Tristan's efforts that he had stood still while Tristan danced around him. On the other hand, although Tristan's feet were leathery and hard, his toes had been cut by the razor-sharp edges of broken shells and, with salt in his wounds, Tristan felt as though he were walking on fire.

Suddenly the lazy Morolt dropped his spear, snatched his axe from its hook on his chest and chopped at the shaft of Tristan's spear. Tristan saw his spearhead dangling and dropped the useless weapon. But immediately Morolt stepped in close, with his axe raised high and with a mighty blow he dented Tristan's helmet, so that Tristan's ears rang. Tristan was dazed and he ducked his head beneath his shield, while he reached for the handle of his sword.

"Crunch!" Morolt's axe buried itself in Tristan's shield-rim. For a moment Morolt's blade was jammed in the wood and copper, and in that instant Tristan drew his sword and brought it down on Morolt's forearm. It was not a powerful blow and Morolt's bracelets took most of the impact but the sharp blade cut into Morolt's wrist and severed the tendons of his thumb. Tristan twisted his shield and wrenched it sideways and Morolt lost his grip on his axe. Nevertheless, however much Tristan shook his head, he could not throw off the singing in his ears and he felt fuddled.

In a moment the sporting contest between two strong and confident men had become a battle between two wounded beasts fighting desperately for their lives. Tristan was no longer fresh and clear-headed, and Morolt was no longer casual. Tristan's face showed the desperate efforts with which he was trying to overcome his dizziness. But Morolt's blue eyes glared furiously; his teeth were bared and the four bedraggled plaits of his red beard were dark with slobber and sweat.

Morolt shifted his shield to his damaged right hand and drew his long sword with his left hand. Tristan should have rushed Morolt at that moment. But he was too dazed to see his chance and busied himself with Morolt's axe which was still stuck in his shield. By the time that Tristan had pulled the axe out and thrown it down, Morolt was advancing to the attack and the ferocious look on Morolt's face showed that he meant to finish the fight at once.

Then for the first time Tristan felt a shiver of dread. The sword in Morolt's hand was longer and heavier than any normal man could wield and Tristan realised that he had never fought or even fenced against a left-handed man. He did not know how to use his shield to deflect a blow coming from his right, and, in defending his head from a hail of blows, he held his shield too high and too far from his body. Suddenly Morolt swung his sword low beneath Tristan's shield. He had meant to strike Tristan's right knee below the byrnie but the big sword was a little too heavy for his weaker left hand and instead, he struck the loosely hanging skirt of Tristan's mail byrnie.

The interlinked iron rings took the brunt of Morolt's blow but the tip of the sharp blade slashed Tristan's leg below the mail. Tristan felt the sting where his flesh was gashed and he felt a tendon part and shrivel up like a snapped bowstring. He stumbled and limped and drew his breath sharply with the pain.

Morolt was quick to seize his advantage in order to make peace, for he was not sure that he could defend himself with a damaged right hand managing his shield and with a sword too heavy for his left hand. So he drew back and asked: "How is it now, Lord Tristan? Have I not proved that my cause is right and that yours is wrong? From that wound you will certainly die, unless I help you. This sword-edge has been wiped with deadly poison, for which there is no cure except a secret ointment known only to my sister, the Queen of Leinster.

"I like you, Tristan and I do not want to cause your death. Come with me to Ireland. I will persuade my sister to heal you and I will share with you all my wealth and pleasures, if only you will bring this fight to an end by acknowledging my right to the tribute."

"I had rather die than shame my reputation with the cowardice of surrender," Tristan answered proudly. "Tonight, Lord Morolt, one of us will be dead. Stroke for stroke I will avenge myself. God defend the right!" Like a boar made savage by the snarling of the hounds around him, Tristan rushed at Morolt; and Morolt found what Tristan had found —that it is difficult to defend oneself when one's shield is not carried on the side from which the blows are coming.

Often Morolt had to use the sword in his left hand to parry Tristan's right-handed attack and more and more the heavy sword tired him. Morolt's defence became slow and clumsy but Tristan felt that victory was within his reach and his eagerness and strength increased tenfold. He struck at Morolt's neck, at his knee, at his elbow, forcing Morolt to shift his guard, and then he swung a mighty blow at Morolt's head. Morolt's sword partly deflected the blow but the crest of his helmet took the weight of it. The iron hat was dashed off his head and fell to the ground with a clang and it rolled, rattling away across the rocks, until it fell into a pool.

As Morolt had turned to get his helmet, he slipped and fell. Tristan sprang forward. His sword parted the sweaty red hair, and cut through skin, bone and brain, until the blade was fully buried in enemy's head. Morolt's sword fell to the rock with a dull clang; his red hair took fresh colour from his blood, and he sagged slowly into a puddle.

Tristan wrenched his sword from the dead man's skull but it was jammed so tightly in the bone that a fragment of the edge broke off, and was left in the wound.

"How is it now, Lord Morolt? Tristan asked. "Have I not proved that my cause is right and that yours is wrong? The wise Queen of Leinster cannot heal that wound."

In order to demonstrate the result of the combat, Tristan cut off Morolt's head and, twisting his fingers through the plaited beard, he tossed the head into the skin-boat in which Morolt had come to the island.

"There is room, after all, for both of us in one boat," said Tristan, as he pushed off.

Tristan let the boat drift with the current, while he washed the splinters of shell from the cuts on his feet and tried desperately to wash the poison from the gash in his thigh. He filled his helmet with sea-water and washed his sweating head and hands and he carefully cleaned his sword-blade, before he sheathed it. Then he took up the oars and rowed not towards the cheering Cornishmen but towards the weeping Irish.

When Tristan was close to where the Irishmen were gathered on the shore, he shouted to them: "Ho there, strangers! Return to your king and take him this tribute from Cornwall."

He picked up Morolt's head by its plaits and flung it, twisting and turning, bouncing and rolling, onto the beach and he shouted again: "Tell your master that, whatever ambassadors he sends here for tribute, we will send them back with as much honour and as much profit as this one."

Tristan had been careful, for his pride's sake, to keep his wound hidden by his shield and the Irishmen assumed that he was unwounded. But Tristan had not noticed that his sword had lost a fragment of its edge and he did not realise that he himself had sent that small piece of iron to the King of Leinster, lodged in Morolt's skull.

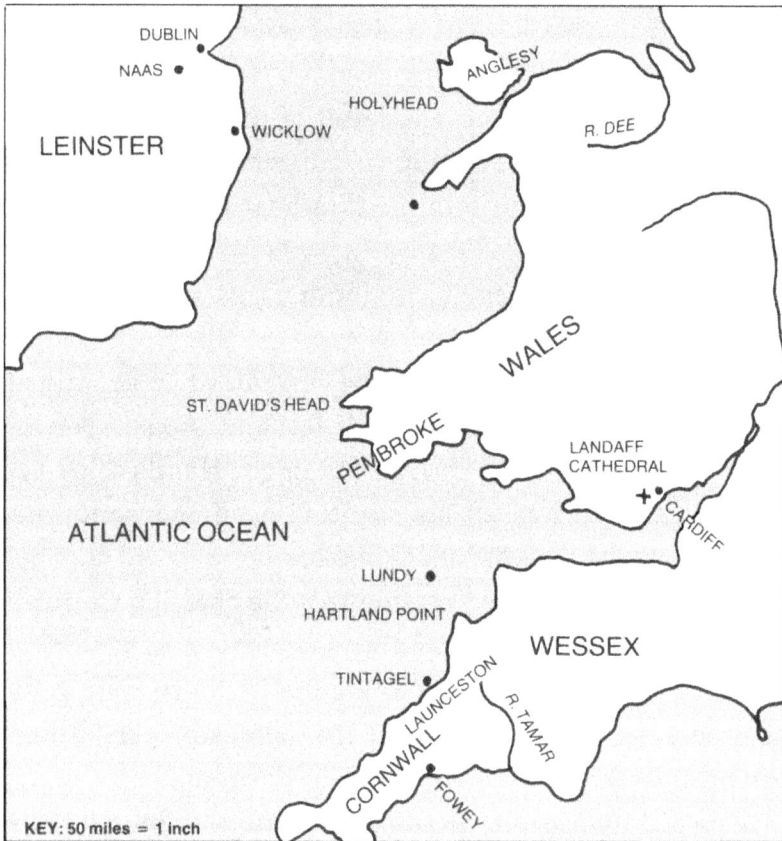

DUBLIN

NAAS

ANGLESY

HOLYHEAD

R. DEE

LEINSTER

WICKLOW

WALES

ST. DAVID'S HEAD

PEMBROKE

LANDAFF
CATHEDRAL

CARDIFF

ATLANTIC OCEAN

LUNDY

HARTLAND POINT

WESSEX

TINTAGEL

LAUNCESTON

R. TAMAR

CORNWALL

FOWEY

KEY: 50 miles = 1 inch

CHAPTER 6

THE MINSTREL

'Tristan! Tristan! Tristan!" the Cornishmen's cheers roared and echoed from the cliffs. The silver sands were brightly embroidered with leaping, waving figures, as the men whom Tristan had saved ran along the shore to greet him. King Mark was weeping, when they embraced, for, truth to tell, he had felt certain that the fearsome Morolt would either kill or maim his beloved nephew. He was astonished and delighted to welcome Tristan back from the fight with only a few scratches on his arms and legs. Only a few scratches! But one had been made by Morolt's poisoned sword.

People were used to wounds and illnesses as trifling nuisances, and that day neither Tristan nor anyone else was much concerned about the wound in his thigh. Wise women scraped the raw flesh, cleaned it with wine (much cleaner than water), closed the wound tightly and bound a plaster on it; and they made Tristan drink a tea brewed with treacle and herbs. They supposed that, if there was any poison in Tristan's wound, the plaster would draw it out and the herb tea would stop it infecting the rest of his body.

When Tristan's wounds had been dressed and when he had been bathed and clothed in costly silks and furs, he was led into the King's hall and King Mark received him with formal ceremony. The King thanked him for rescuing the people of Cornwall from the shameful tribute which they had suffered for so long and he declared, so that all in his court could hear him: "Now I am altogether sure, Tristan, that by right both of blood and of excellence you ought to be my heir, and all the chiefs of Cornwall here assembled will uphold my choice. I call upon the Great Men of Cornwall to do obedient homage to Tristan as my heir."

Some of the Cornish chiefs were reluctant to accept as their lord a man whom they regarded as a foreigner but their own failings had been clearly revealed and their wives and kinsmen were grateful to Tristan for saving their children from slavery. Therefore the chiefs swore to honour Tristan as the King's son and to accept him as King of Cornwall when King Mark died, unless the King got a lawful son and heir. And King Mark announced that he intended to remain unmarried and childless, in order that Tristan might be sure of the succession.

The Cornish chieftains resolved in their hearts never to accept Tristan as King of Cornwall, for they begrudged his virtues and, although openly they honoured him, really they hated him for exposing their cowardice. But the King and the simple people were very grateful to him and treated him like a well-loved hero. They were anxious, when his limp became worse and they mourned, when his cheeks became pale and his flesh melted away.

Soon Tristan noticed that, whenever he was in the King's hall, the courtiers gathered at the far end and he saw that the King, beside whom he sat, often turned his head away and sniffed at an orange stuffed with herbs. Tristan felt deserted and he no longer thought it worthwhile to undergo the pain and weariness of getting dressed and walking to the hall. He stayed in the bed in his beehive-shaped sleeping-hut and, when he had the strength, he consoled himself with singing and harping.

The dreadful truth was that Tristan stank. His wound festered; his right leg was discoloured and shrunken from the knee to the groin and his whole body was nothing but skin and bone. The wise women and doctors of Cornwall and Wales were summoned and tried their remedies, hoping to draw the poison from Tristan's wound but all failed utterly.

The greatest service which could be done for Tristan was to turn his frail body and to empty out the stinking pus which always collected in his open wound. This service was so unpleasant that his friends were reluctant to visit him, for fear of being asked to do it. In the end only his faithful Master was willing to sit with him and Tristan passed the time disputing with Master about learned matters and listening while Master read aloud the books which merchants brought from distant lands.

One day, Tristan sent Master to ask King Mark to visit him. Before the King arrived, Tristan's wound was cleaned and rosemary was burnt, in order to sweeten the air of his cell but the place still stank. King Mark tried to ignore the foul stench of putrefaction and decay, because he did not want to hurt his nephew but he could not keep his hand from his face and he held his nose with his scented robe.

"Lord King!" said Tristan, "if you love me truly, give me comfort in my grievous life and give me counsel in my difficulty. My former friends no longer visit me and I lack the strength to visit them. All the doctors of Cornwall and Wales have failed to cure my sickness and I am a living corpse, an offence to my friends, an abomination to myself. If I stay here, I shall certainly die, for here I have no hope of cure. Therefore I wish to go away and I ask your help.

"Morolt told me that his sword was wiped with a poison for which only his sister, the Queen of Leinster, knows the cure. Therefore I propose to sail to Ireland and to try to obtain her help."

"But, Nephew!" King Mark protested, "The Irish hate us even more than they hate the Devil. I have heard that the Queen has sworn vengeance against you for killing her brother and the King of

Leinster has given orders that every living thing which comes from Cornwall, whether it is man or beast, must be killed on arrival."

"Nevertheless, Uncle, to a dying man the likelihood of a quick death causes joy rather than fear. I mean to try my luck and to pray for God's help. Please find me a small ship with a crew of foreigners, who will hold their tongues for gold, and let it be widely known that I am going to Spain to seek help from the clever Moorish doctors."

Since King Mark knew of no better solution to Tristan's problem, he reluctantly agreed to the desperate plan and, when Tristan told his Master what he intended, Master insisted on accompanying him on the voyage. One evening in the dusk Tristan was carried aboard a Breton trading ship and Master went with him. They sailed in the dark and King Mark gave it out that Tristan had gone to Spain, hoping to be cured by the Morish doctors of Cordova.

The simple people wept and prayed God to help the unfortunate man who had suffered so much for Cornwall's sake. Most of the chiefs were very pleased to be rid of the foreigner who had been put over them and Tristan's companions were relieved to be freed from the duty of visiting their smelly leader.

Meanwhile, Tristan's ship made for Ireland and Tristan told the captain to set a course for Dublin, keeping away from land to avoid being reported. One evening they saw Dublin in the distance and anchored till night. When it was quite dark, Tristan told the captain to take the ship in towards the shore, as near as he safely could, and to anchor there until the ebb-tide turned. By the time that the tide was setting strongly towards the shore, it was nearly dawn and Tristan told the captain to lower a small boat and to put him in it with his harp and enough food and water for three days.

Master wanted to come too but Tristan said: "Dear Master, I believe that my plan is more likely to succeed if I am on my own and I should not like to risk your life, when mine is of so little value. I want you to ensure that these seamen are well rewarded for their trouble and that they swear solemnly to keep my secret. Tell my uncle that I hope to return whole and healthy before winter and ask him to hold my men and goods until a year has passed. If I do not come back to Cornwall within a year, you and my Lothian friends must go home to Edinburgh. Tell Marshal Ronald my news and tell him that my last wish was that he should treat you very generously, for you deserve it."

Not only Master but the Breton seamen too were weeping but Tristan commanded the captain: "Now cast me adrift and take my master back to Tintagel. When people ask what happened to me, tell them that I died on the journey to Spain, for I shall be a dead man if the Queen of Leinster hears that I am in Ireland. If you obey my orders, you will be well rewarded."

The seamen cut the painter which held Tristan's boat; they weighed their anchor and they set their sail. The ship bowed before the breeze and she slipped away like a ghost into the darkness. "God keep you!" Master cried through his tears. "God bless you!" came the chorus of rough sailor's voices. "God save my soul and give you good weather!" Tristan answered. But the ship was already beyond the range of Tristan's feeble voice and he drifted alone on the empty face of the unfriendly sea, heaving on the swell, spinning with every breeze, utterly helpless and at the mercy of wind and water.

Tristan had calculated that the incoming tide and the morning breeze would carry his boat towards the shore and he hoped to reach land near the village of Dublin, the primitive port of the King of Leinster. As he lay in the bottom of his boat, he could see neither land nor sea but, when daylight dawned and colour flooded the sky above him, he began to play his harp, for he relied on music to attract attention. Sure enough! It was not long before he saw a bearded face looking over the gunnel of his boat. Another face joined it and another and another.

"Welcome, stranger!" the four boatmen said politely. "What brings you here, looking so ill and playing so well?"

"Masters, I am a minstrel, as you can see," said Tristan. "But, instead of being content with the gold which my music earned me, I was persuaded to put all that I owned into a trading venture. Then, when we were at sea with a rich cargo of goods, sea-robbers boarded us. They took our ship and all our goods and they killed every man in the ship except me. Although I was wounded, they spared my life, because I am a minstrel, for many people believe that to kill a minstrel brings bad luck.

"The robbers cast me adrift in this small boat. Since then, for God knows how many days, I have wandered helpless on the sea, a plaything of the winds and waves and I have often wished that I had been killed along with the others, because my life has been so miserable and my pain so great."

"You are in luck, minstrel!" one of the Irish boatmen said cheerfully. "For you have reached land and in this country we value minstrels highly."

"Good master, please do not mock me," Tristan begged. "Tell me the truth. Where in the world am I? And from what country do you come?"

"Good minstrel, you have reached Ireland and we are Leinstermen. We put out from shore, to salvage, as we thought, an empty boat drifting without an owner."

"Masters, if you will tow me to some place where there are people, you may have my boat freely and forever, for I hope to be able to earn my bed and board by playing and singing."

"Agreed, Minstrel. We will tow you to our town, which lies nearby and, if you play your harp while we pull our oars, some rich man may hear you and give you lodging."

The boatmen secured a line to both boats and rowed towards the town. The townspeople, who were coming from their houses to start the day's work, were surprised to hear sweet music coming from an apparently empty boat, for, although Tristan played and sang with newfound hope, he was still lying flat in the bottom of his boat. When the boatmen pulled Tristan's boat up onto the shore, the townspeople flocked to see the wonder, and they were astonished when they saw that the minstrel who sang and harped so well was more dead than alive.

"What town is this?" Tristan asked innocently. "And is anyone here kind enough to help me?"

"This is Dublin, minstrel," the townsmen answered. "But we do not know whether anyone here can help a man in such trouble as you seem to be. Tell us your story."

Again and again to each new group of sightseers, Tristan told his story and he took care to tell it the same every time. Each visitor asked him to play or to sing a song, to prove that he was indeed a minstrel and all declared that he sang and harped like an angel straight from heaven. Soon all the town was talking about the wonderful minstrel who had been carried by wind and wave right to their door and it was not long before it was freely said that God Himself had brought the minstrel, to give them comfort in their grief at Morolt's death.

At last the town elders, seeing Tristan so utterly helpless and yet so bravely making music, asked their doctor to take him into his house and they promised to pay for whatever treatment the doctor thought might save Tristan's life. Tristan was carried from his boat to the doctor's house and the doctor gave him what treatment he could. But nothing the doctor did made Tristan's wound any less painful or any less rotten and his house was crowded with people asking Tristan to sing or play for them. Tristan played willingly but he was becoming weaker and ever weaker, and the doctor thought that Tristan could not last many more days.

Among the visitors who came to hear the castaway musician was a certain priest, who was himself a distinguished harpist and he was much impressed both by Tristan's skill as a minstrel and by the courage with which he played for others' pleasure, even though he was dying. That priest was confessor to the Queen of Leinster and tutor to her daughter, twelve-year-old Isolt.

The priest hurried to the King of Leinster's dun, a few miles away at Naas, and told the Queen: "Lady, today in Dublin town I saw a wonder such as I never thought to see. A young minstrel arrived one night adrift in a boat, not knowing where in the world he was and he is so ill that there is not an ounce of flesh on his bones. He is the most talented singer and harpist whom I have ever heard. But the doctor says that he is bound to die soon.

"It is a great pity, Lady, that you cannot hear him, for you cannot go to Dublin and he cannot travel here. When I heard him sing and play so sweetly in spite of all his pain and weakness, I thought: *What wonderful music he would play, if he were in good health! What a rare teacher he would be for the fair princess! What a pity that he has to die, before the Gracious Queen has even heard him!*"

The Queen was famous for her skill in medicine and the priest's words had whetted her curiosity. She asked sharply: "What is his illness? Has he got boils or a rash? Does he cough blood? Is he feverish? What dreadful disease should I catch, if I was foolish enough to go near him?"

"To all appearances, Lady, he has no disease nor any illness except what is caused by a septic wound in his leg. He says that he was wounded by the sea-robbers who captured his ship and turned him adrift. The doctor cannot heal the rotten flesh around the wound and not only the minstrel's thigh-bone but his whole body is being poisoned by the putrefaction. The doctor says that the poor man is so feeble that he must die soon."

"I never in my life saw any leg wound which I could not heal," the Queen said proudly and she gave orders for the sick minstrel to be brought in a litter to a hut near her hall.

"If I can heal him, we shall have a teacher for my daughter Isolt. If I fail, we may hear him play before he dies," the Queen said. But she added confidently, "I never yet had a patient who died of a wound in the arm or leg. The doctor must have tried the wrong remedy."

The next day, when Tristan was lying exhausted by the pain of being moved to the royal dun at Naas, the Queen came to see him. He tried to sit up in bed but he could hardly raise his head. So he placed his hands palm to palm in a gesture of respect. The Queen told the priest to repeat Tristan's story but during the telling she carefully watched Tristan's skull-like face and at the end she asked him sternly whether the priest had told the story truly. Tristan nodded and, when she asked whether all his illness was caused by the wound in his leg, he whispered: "To tell you the truth, Gracious Lady, I do not know. I supposed that my body was feeble and my wound septic because of my long time adrift on the sea."

"Let me see the wound," the Queen said and, when she had examined first of all the wound and then the swollen gland in the groin, the shrivelled muscles and crumbling thigh-bone, she declared, "The weapon which made this wound was poisoned."

"Poisoned, Lady?" Tristan asked with pretended surprise. "I never heard that Norse robbers used poison."

"If the man who wounded you was a Norseman, he probably used eel-juice, for that is a poison much used in Norway," the Queen said thoughtfully. "I have the remedy for it, stranger," she added. "But, before I undertake to cure you, I want to know who you are and where you come from and what trade you follow."

"Lady, my name is Tantris. I am a Breton from Rennes and misfortune struck me because I was greedy. I am a minstrel who plays every stringed instrument known in the western world. But foolishly I tried to grow rich by trading."

"If you have the strength, Tantris, I should like to hear the proof of your claim to be a minstrel. I shall not make you play all the instruments which you claim. It will be enough if you will harp for me and my young daughter."

"Willingly, Gracious Lady," he answered.

Tristan asked for his harp and, after tuning it carefully, he played a melody, which was full of the hope in his heart. Then, feeling stronger, he sang a song about the joy of spring after the pinching cold of winter. The Princess Isolt was enchanted. Nevertheless, at the end of the song she hurried from the hut, to escape from the stench of Tristan's putrid flesh.

"Tantris," said the Queen. "If I can purge your wound of the stinking decay, so that people can bear to sit with you, will you teach my daughter the harp? If you agree, I undertake to heal your wound and to make you well."

"Gracious Lady, I count myself cured already," Tristan said happily. "Whatever arts of music or book-learning I know, I will gladly try to teach them to your fair daughter."

Thus it happened that Tristan was well received by Morolt's sister, who had sworn an oath to be revenged on him and thus it happened that he first met Isolt, with whom his life-thread later became inextricably entangled. Morolt's sister cured his poisoned wound and in a few months brought him back to health and Isolt, a slim, fair-haired girl of twelve, became his pupil.

Isolt could already play the harp but Tristan improved her harping and taught her to play the fiddle as well. He taught her many pleasant pieces for both instruments and he taught her many noble songs for a girl's voice. She already spoke Irish (for her father was Irish), Norse (for her mother was Norse,) and some Latin, which was the language of the Christian Gospels and the Holy

Offices, but Tristan taught her also polite phrases in English, Frankish and Breton.

King Angus, Isolt's father, doted upon her, for she was his only child, with golden hair and the lanky beauty of a deer. He liked to summon her into his hall after supper, when the mead-cup was going round among his guests and chieftains. At her father's command she would play or sing or read aloud from a book or answer the men's questions and riddles.

When Isolt had had lessons from Tristan for six months, the King could not allow two nights to pass without calling her to entertain his hall, for her range of skills had doubled and there were very few visitors from foreign lands whom she could not address in their own tongue. Also, in those six months she had grown six months nearer to her full womanly beauty and many idle minds around her father's hall were full of thoughts about her. For that reason the applause for her performance always pleased her father; her fame spread like a heath-fire and her reputation outshone even her truly remarkable accomplishments.

After six months in Ireland Tristan had regained full health and strength and his face had filled out so much that he was afraid of being recognised by one of Morolt's men. To disguise himself, he now shaved every day, whereas previously he had let his beard grow and he wore long robes of black or brown, whereas previously he had worn short tunics of bright colours plus linen trousers in the winter. Now he was as anxious to leave Ireland as he had previously been to reach it— and for the same reason— to save his life.

One day Tristan knelt humbly before the Queen and her daughter and, after singing a song in praise of their charm, he said: "Ladies most fair, although I am only poor, I shall always make it my duty to praise you in the hearing of rich men and I ask God Himself to reward you properly for what you have done for me. By your leave, Gracious Queen, I want to go home, for I am in full health, thanks to your kindness and healing skill and I ought to comfort my family and friends, who must suppose me dead."

"Against your two reasons, Tantris my friend, I set two stronger arguments," the Queen replied. "My daughter needs you to teach her and I do not propose to lose my best minstrel, until he has served me for the customary year."

"Gracious and Noble Lady! Remember the sacred ties of marriage and parenthood. Imagine the temptations of my wife, whom I love dearly, and of her father, whose right and duty it is to give her to another man if he believes me dead," cried Tristan, so anxiously that the Queen believed him. "Think, dear lady, of the agony which I should endure if I returned to find my darling wife married to someone else. Noble Queen, let your own heart persuade you to let me go."

The Queen grumbled, "It is always the same, when one helps a stranger. As soon as new friendships are formed and new bonds of loyal service are tied, the pull of kith and kin tears friendships and loyalties apart. But I cannot deny that the ties of holy wedlock are stronger than those which bind master and servant, tutor and pupil, doctor and patient.   With a good will but a reluctant heart, Tantris, I give you leave. My treasurer will give you a pennyweight of gold from me for travelling expenses and a second gold penny from my daughter for your future upkeep."

Tristan joined his hands and bowed his face almost to the floor, first to the Queen and then to her daughter and humbly and sincerely he took his leave. "Gracious Ladies, may God give you honour as much as I shall ever give you thanks!"

Tristan took ship to Wales, and from Wales he sailed to Tintagel. Even before Tristan landed, ever-watchful Master had recognised him standing in the stern and the one word "Tristan" sped from mouth to mouth up the rocky shore to the King's palace, until the whole camp heaved like an ant-heap. Men and women, chiefs and peasants, warriors and priests, even the King himself, ran to meet the boat which brought Tristan to land. It seemed a miracle that Tristan, who had left them looking more like a corpse than a living man, should return to them so handsome and so strong.

That day the King gave a joyful feast and, in welcoming Tristan back, he told his courtiers, "Now I know for certain that God intends Tristan to be my heir and King of Cornwall after my days are done."

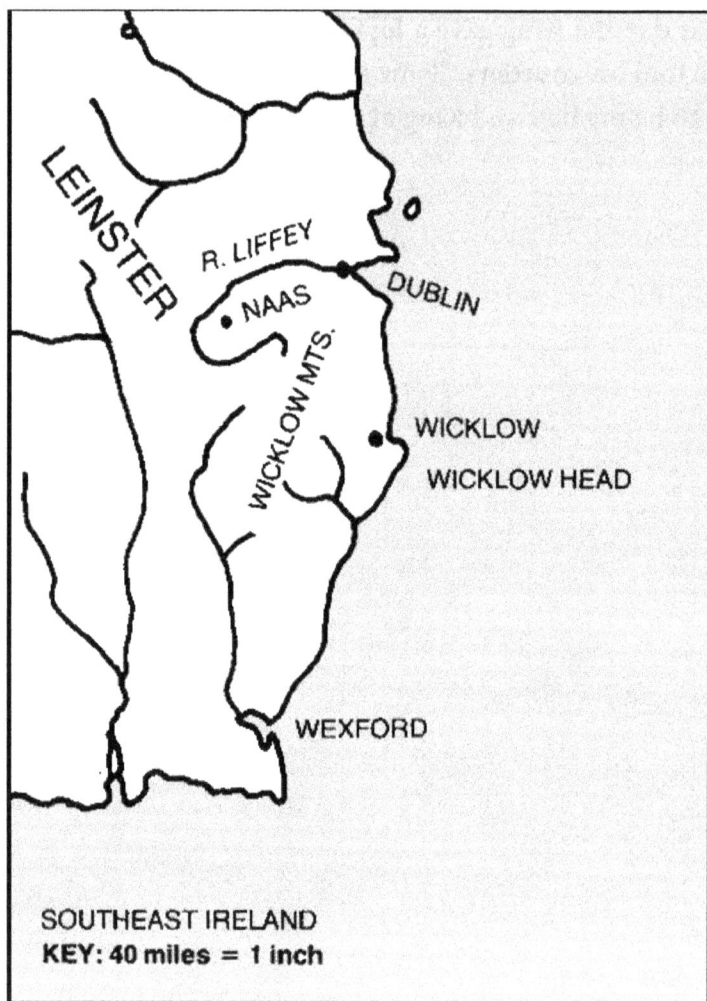

LEINSTER

R. LIFFEY

NAAS

DUBLIN

WICKLOW MTS.

WICKLOW

WICKLOW HEAD

WEXFORD

SOUTHEAST IRELAND
KEY: 40 miles = 1 inch

CHAPTER 7

THE DRAGON

Throughout the winter King Mark cherished and indulged Tristan and rejoiced to see him so well. Again and again the courtiers made Tristan tell his story and he related how he had tricked Morolt's sister into healing his wound, although she would rather have killed him if she had known who he was. Nevertheless, Tristan kept his promise to his benefactors and he praised them to the sky. The Queen of Leinster he likened to the colourful dawn but Isolt, the princess, he likened to the golden sun and he declared that within a year Isolt's beauty would be so dazzling that all other lights would seem dull by comparison. "Isolt the Fair, Isolt the Sun, her beauty dazzles everyone. Isolt the Sun, Isolt the Fair, sheds golden glory everywhere," he sang.

Nor did Tristan neglect to praise the accomplishments of the two beautiful ladies. He said that the Queen of Leinster was the wisest woman and the most learned doctor in the West, and that Isolt was a paragon of musicianship and skilful conversation.

To the people of King Mark's court, penned in their dark and crowded buildings by the stinging whip of the winter wind, it seemed as though Tristan had visited the Otherworld, for the two great ladies sounded as lovely as the deathless fairies of the Isle of

Women. During the stormy days and long winter nights many dreams were woven around Tristan's tales and some people wondered whether Tristan himself had some fairy powers, for what he had achieved seemed humanly impossible.

When the Cornish chiefs were summoned to Tintagel for the Easter feast, Tristan was sitting at the King's side and the King and his courtiers did whatever Tristan wanted, as though he was already king. Some of the chiefs begrudged Tristan his good looks, his courage and his luck, and they envied him King Mark's love and his popularity with the simple people. They put it about that Tristan was a witch.

"How else," they said, "could he have defeated that giant Morolt? How else could he have made Morolt's sister heal him? And is it not obvious that he has bewitched King Mark? Have you ever seen a king so besotted, so humble and so obedient as Mark? Tristan might be the King's own son instead of the bastard of a Pictish barbarian."

During the eight-day feast, the Cornish chiefs, one after another spoke to King Mark about marrying to get an heir but he always said: "God has preserved Tristan for us in spite of many dangers and I pray that He will keep Tristan safe to rule Cornwall after my death. God has sent us an excellent heir and I don't need a queen."

Because they were thwarted, the Cornish chiefs began to mutter and to speak openly of their hatred of Tristan and, when King Mark told the priest to add Tristan's name to his own in the prayer for the safety of the Royal Family, some chiefs prayed for Tristan's death. Soon Tristan noticed that even his sworn companions found it difficult to smile in his eyes, for they were the sons of Cornish chiefs and he often noticed scowling groups of men plotting in corners.

"In God's name, Uncle!" Tristan said to King Mark, "Consider how the chiefs dislike me, because you will not marry. They blame it all on me, and I am beginning to be afraid that I may soon die of poisoned food or an assassin's knife."

"Don't talk such nonsense, Tristan," King Mark answered sternly. "So long as you are alive, I want no heir but you and, while you are my companion, I need no queen. Do not be afraid of my scowling chiefs. You are quite safe, while under my protection.

"You cannot avoid jealousy, Tristan," the King said. "Every good man suffers from the envy of others. Everyone who is successful, whether through skill or through good luck attracts the envy of those who are less skilful or less lucky. Whatever people say: hold your head high; decide what best serves your honour and advantage, and then stick to it."

But Tristan insisted: "I should rather be a landless wanderer than rule the earth in such discomfort as I now feel, Sire, and since I cannot be happy in such an atmosphere of hatred and spite, 1 ask permission to leave your court."

King Mark was shocked and distressed by the suggestion and he said plaintively, "Tristan, it is because of my love and loyalty that I want _you_ to be my heir. But, if you will not have it so, what do you wish me to do?"

"Summon your council, Sire and find out what they want. Then, provided that they seek your honour, try to make them happy by following their advice."

When the Cornish chiefs were assembled in council, they all with one voice advised the King to marry and they advised him to beget an heir with a lawful wife, so that they could have for their lord and king a Cornishman born and bred.

"I thank you for your good will, lords and councillors," said King Mark; "for I see that with this advice you seek my honour and my worship. You tell me to marry, in order that my blood may rule

Cornwall after my own death but I can assure you that I will not marry any woman unless she is my equal both in birth and in rank, good-looking and also well brought up. If you know of a suitable maiden whom I can marry without loss of honour, I will think about it."

The chiefs pretended to confer, although the plotters had already decided what name to suggest. Then their leader stepped forward and said: "Sire, you have often heard of a beautiful and accomplished girl, like you of royal blood and heir to a kingdom. We propose that you should seek the hand of Fair Isolt, the King of Leinster's daughter. Tristan, your nephew, will bear us witness that in all the world there is no bride more suitable."

The King smiled at this suggestion, for it seemed to him impossible that the King of Leinster would marry his daughter to his mortal enemy. "King Angus would rather kill me than give me his daughter. For there has not been a kind thought between us for many years," he said. "If I sent an ambassador to Leinster, he would be ill-treated and probably killed; my request would be refused with ignominy and I should be laughed at by all the world. How should I gain honour and worship from <u>that</u>?"

The King laughed scornfully, dismissing the proposal but the chiefs reasoned, "Sire, it often happens that two kings are at odds for a long time. But sometimes, with good will on both sides, the quarrel is made up and a marriage is made between their children. When the two kings are related by marriage and their blood is mingled in darling grandchildren, old hatreds are forgotten and peace reigns. Bear in mind, Sire, that the Lady Isolt is King Angus' only child, the heir to his kingdom. He needs to find a strong husband for her, because someday the man who marries her must enforce her claim and rule her inheritance. Sire, would you not gain great honour and worship, if Leinster were added to Cornwall under your rule?"

The King sat quietly, considering what to say. He still thought that the Irish marriage was unattainable but for that very reason he calculated that he could safely accept his chiefs' advice and still keep Tristan for his heir. Suddenly he spoke: "Lords, you have convinced me. Since your proposal is intended to enhance my honour and worship, I will marry Isolt and no one else, for, as you say, the Lady Isolt is my equal in blood and possessions and, after hearing Tristan's stories of her beauty and charm, her wit and accomplishments, I am quite in love with her. Yes! I swear by God and by my life that, if I cannot have Isolt, I will have no wife at all."

The chiefs were pleased when they saw how readily the King fell in with their scheme and, when he asked, "But how do you suggest that the Lady Isolt should be wooed for my wife?" they all shouted eagerly, "Tristan! The Lord Tristan can fetch the Lady. He knows the country and the language and he is a friend of both the Lady Isolt and her mother. Send Tristan, Sire. By hook or by crook, by skill or by luck, he will get her for you. He never fails, that one."

The King was shocked and very angry. "You wicked men! You evil counsellors!" he shouted. "I can see your purpose. But I am not cruel enough to send my nephew to certain death. The Queen of Leinster has sworn to kill him and the King of Leinster has forbidden Cornishmen to set foot in his land. Tristan is hated in Ireland and fair game for any rogue who can catch him. Tristan has risked his life to save you and he has only just recovered from his grievous wounds. You can go yourselves, you ungrateful wretches. And don't come back, unless you bring me the Lady Isolt."

The chiefs looked anxiously at one another. They shifted their feet and cursed "that witch Tristan" beneath their breath.

Tristan saw that the King had the chiefs at his mercy because he had accepted their own advice and had commanded them to carry it out. But he could also see that the frustrated chiefs would go on hating him until the King had got a son and heir. Tristan's interests were many and varied, but he had no interest in possessions nor in the tiresome chores of government. He was quite willing to give up his inheritance for the sake of popularity, especially when there was an adventure in view.

"Lord King!" he said. "In my opinion these noble chiefs have advised you well. It is true that in the whole wide world no lady is better fitted to be your bride and queen than the Lady Isolt. Your honour and power would be much increased by marriage to the heiress of Leinster. It is also true that I can speak Irish and that I know the King of Leinster and his chiefs, the noble Queen and her incomparable daughter, Fair Isolt. Nevertheless, Sire, I slew Morolt, the Queen's brother and the King's champion, who came here to enslave the sons of these noble chiefs and both the Queen and her fair daughter have sworn to kill me if they can. Because of this disability I may lose my life and therefore fail you, Sire. It is a very good thing that you have commanded these noble chiefs to accompany me to Ireland, for, if I fail, they may still succeed and, if I succeed, they will add to my embassy both weight and dignity and will be a token that your desire for peace is fully shared by all the men of Cornwall."

The chiefs had been uneasy at the prospect of going to Ireland instead of Tristan but they were terrified of going there with him, for they knew that he was hated in Ireland and they expected that not only Tristan but all in his company would be put to death most painfully. However, they were caught in their own snare and they could not escape it.

King Mark was deeply distressed that Tristan had insisted on going to Ireland, for he was a lonely man and Tristan was his only friend. "God has saved you from the Irish devils twice, nephew" he said. "It is flying in His face to deliver yourself into their power yet again."

"Do not despair, Sire," Tristan said cheerfully. "It is an adventure and perhaps I shall bring you back great honour and worship with the Lady Isolt. If I do not bring you the Lady, I shall not return at all. But, if I should fail, I shall leave your honour and worship safely in the hands of these excellent chiefs, who think only of your interests."

Tristan hired three wooden ships with their Frisian crews and he embarked his Master, twenty of his sworn companions, twenty of the Cornish chiefs and sixty archers and spearmen. The King had no fear for the cowardly chiefs for he knew that they would manage to avoid danger. But he parted from Tristan with a very sad heart, because he thought that he had seen the last of his adventurous nephew, who alone of all the world had found a soft spot in his heart.

During the voyage Tristan was light-hearted, though he was by nature not at all merry and he kept asking the chiefs' advice on how to woo the Irish princess. The more Tristan asked for advice and declared that he himself had no idea how to win the girl, the more frightened the chiefs became but the bravest of them advised the others: "Leave it to Tristan. He is a clever fellow, with the Devil's own luck. Trust him to bring us safely out of our difficulties. Only pray to God that he does nothing rash because he seems to be completely fearless."

The ships' captains laid a course past Lundy Island to the Pembroke coast and, when they had rounded Saint David's Head, they altered course, to make a landfall on the east coast of Ireland. Even when the Irish coast appeared ahead of them, Tristan had not thought how to bring his adventure to a successful end, but the moment that the Frisian captain recognised their landfall and shouted: "Wicklow Head!" Tristan's eyes shone. "That's it," he muttered and ordered the captain: "Put in towards Wicklow but drop anchor outside the harbour."

"Now, my friends, we are in Irish waters," Tristan told his fellow ambassadors. "So all Cornishmen must stay out of sight if they hope to stay alive. My Master and I will take an eight-oared boat towards the town and we shall try to obtain permission to anchor in the harbour and to trade here. If you see us killed, you had better sail away. Meanwhile, spread the ships' awnings and no one except the crew must show himself."

Tristan and Master put on dark capes, such as merchants wore and they were rowed towards the town by eight strong Frisian seamen. As they drew near the town, they saw armed men running down to the shore and Tristan hailed them: "Ahoy there! Have we permission to land? "

"Come in close, so that I can have a look at you," answered the leader of the armed men. "I am the King's reeve and I want to know who you are and where you come from, and where you are going and what is your purpose. This is Morolt's town and we kill anyone who stinks of Cornwall."

"By my faith!" said Tristan. "We are Breton traders and we sailed from Brittany. We had intended to trade in Wales, but there was a storm and we were swept way off our course. We have put in here, hoping to repair the storm-damage but we can sell you wheat and flour and we would like to buy gold-dust and hides."

One of the Frisian seamen cried out in alarm and Tristan saw that a fleet of skin-boats had put out from shore in order to surround him. "Call your boats in, Master Reeve," he warned; "or I shall signal my ships to sail away and then your king will lose his harbour dues."

"What will you pay the King, if I let you shelter in our harbour?"

"I will pay the King a pennyweight of gold for every day that we stay, good reeve, and if you can guarantee the safety of myself, my men, my ships and goods, you can have this gold cup for yourself."

The sight of the gold cup persuaded the port reeve and in the

King's name he commanded the people of Wicklow neither to rob nor to harm the strangers. Then Tristan signalled to his ships that they could anchor in the sheltered harbour and he returned aboard for the night.

The reason why Tristan had put in to Wicklow, although that had been Morolt's town, was that he had remembered the Dragon of Wicklow. While Tristan had been masquerading as a minstrel and living in the King of Leinster's dun at Naas, he had heard about an age-old dragon, which lived in the Wicklow Mountains and he had heard that, when Isolt was still a small child, the King had promised to give her in marriage to any man who could kill the dragon. As Isolt grew older and more beautiful and yet remained the King's only child, more and more brave or ambitious men had tried to kill the dragon, but found their own death. It was said that during its long life the dragon had killed thousands of warriors without ever being hurt.

Tristan had been told that the dragon usually hunted at daybreak, and during the night when all the Cornishmen were fast asleep, Tristan woke his Master and the captain of the ship. He told them to land him and to wait for a week. If by then they had no news of him, he said, they should go home.

Tristan was rowed ashore at a place where there were no houses, and he climbed a hill overlooking the town, in the hope of hearing or seeing where the dragon was hunting that morning, as he wanted to follow the beast to its lair. Even before the eastern sky had been coloured by the dawn, Tristan heard a terrible roaring and the shouts and screams of terrified men and women. Then he saw flames rising from a house on the outskirts of Wicklow and the townspeople swarming like ants down to the seashore and either jumping into boats or wading up to their necks in the sea.

Tristan did not see the dragon, for the dragon had taken its dinner from the house which it had destroyed and had escaped into the dark countryside. But Tristan soon found where the dragon had broken through the town's stockade, and he also found a frightened horse running loose. He mounted the horse and he rode him bareback, with his hand entwined in his mane and with his spear for a whip.

As Tristan followed the track of the dragon, four armed warriors galloped towards him. "Fly, man! Fly for your life!" they shouted but they did not draw rein. Tristan beat his horse the harder, for he thought that the dragon could not be far away. He was right. Suddenly he saw it close in front of him. At the same instant it turned and saw him.

Tristan held his shield over the horse's eyes and drew back his spear. The dragon opened its jaws and belched out a cloud of stinking smoke. Tristan flung his spear with all his strength into the cavern of the dragon's mouth, straight down its throat. Then horse and man and armour-plated dragon collided with a crash which hurled both Tristan and his mount sprawling onto the ground.

Fortunately for Tristan, the dragon pounced on the horse and bit off its head, and when it tried to swallow the head, it felt the spear-point stuck deep in its gullet. The wounded dragon bellowed with pain and turned for home. Tristan followed on foot. He could not keep up with the big beast but it was so inflamed with rage and pain that, wherever it went, it scorched the grass and Tristan easily tracked it to its lair in the hills.

The beast lay in its cave, facing the entrance and, when Tristan advanced to attack it, it blew out flames. Tristan's wooden shield was charred in spite of the copper facing; his rawhide leg-straps and linen trousers were scorched and the iron rings of his mail shirt became painfully hot. But the beast's breath became less fiery; its eyes closed and it lay shaking and shivering in its death-agony. When Tristan advanced again, the beast made no move to attack him and he crept past its terrible head and drove his sword up to the hilt into its heart.

When the dragon felt the sharp steel at its life-centre, it uttered a shriek louder and more terrible than any which Tristan had ever heard. Tristan was afraid that the dragon's death-cry might bring sightseers to the place and he did not want to be seen. With his sword he prised open the beast's jaws, and with his knife he cut off its tongue. He concealed the tongue inside his shirt, sheathed his sword and closed the dragon's mouth and then he hurried away, to hide until nightfall, when he could go back to his friends without being seen.

Although Tristan was running downhill, he felt utterly weary; his head was spinning and his body felt as though it was on fire. Before him he saw a pool, where a hill-stream ran into a marsh and he could think of nothing but the coolness of water to sooth his itching skin. He threw off his helmet and shield and lay down full-length in the pool, with his head pillowed on a rock at the water's edge, and then he fainted.

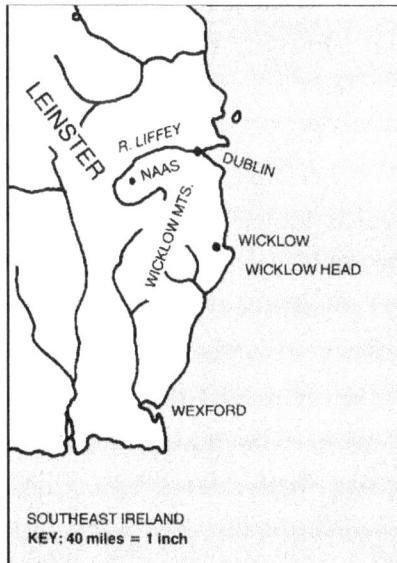

LEINSTER
R. LIFFEY
NAAS
DUBLIN
WICKLOW MTS.
WICKLOW
WICKLOW HEAD
WEXFORD

SOUTHEAST IRELAND
KEY: 40 miles = 1 inch

CHAPTER 8

THE FALSE CLAIMANT

Tristan lay unconscious for a night, a day, and a second night. Then the mists which clouded his mind began to disperse and he heard excited voices, like sparrows chattering. He was sweating and feverish hot but he felt gentle hands, like the fluttering of butterfly wings, on his forehead and chest. He heard a woman's voice: "This man is going to live. The theriac with which I dosed him is making him sweat and the poison in his chest is already yielding its grip on his heart. He will soon come round."

Tristan blinked and opened his eyes, to see his rescuers and then he muttered: "Ah! Merciful God! Thou hast not forgotten me." For the three women who were bending over him were the Queen of Leinster, the Lady Isolt and their cousin the Lady Bronwen. To Tristan they seemed like the Bright Dawn, the Noonday Sun and the Full Moon, for he wanted to see those three women more than anyone else in the world. However, he acted his part and whispered: "Who are you? Where am I?"

Tristan closed his eyes, as if he had fainted again. But he heard Isolt say, "I believe that this is Tantris the Minstrel." He felt a hand pull at his trousers and he heard the Queen say with a surprised laugh, "Yes! It is Tantris. I recognise that scar on his thigh." The women and their squire lifted Tristan onto a horse but he knew no more, for his mind had slipped back into the darkness.

When Tristan woke up the next morning, the Queen and Isolt were sitting by his bed and the Queen asked, "Are you strong enough to talk, Tantris? I want to know why you are in Ireland and whether you were concerned in any way with the dragon's death."

Tristan answered: "I took a share in a trading venture, Gracious Queen and a storm drove us into Wicklow but the people there were so hostile that I had to give the King's Reeve a large present to secure our safety. I decided to earn the favour and protection of the Noble King himself by killing the dragon which I had heard about while I was here last year. So I hunted it to its lair and killed it; but I fainted, before I could get back to my companions and now I believe, Dear and Gracious Lady, that I owe my life to you for the second time."

"You do indeed, Tantris but the King and I, and also my daughter Isolt, are much obliged to you for killing that dragon and you have earned the favour and protection which you sought. I myself will guarantee your safety."

Tristan looked doubtful about the value of a woman's protection and he said, "I hope, Lady, that I need never regret that you have made yourself responsible for my safety and I hope that my men, my ships and my goods will be free from trouble in your care."

"I give you my hand on it, Tantris," said the Queen. "So long as I live, you and your men and your belongings will be safe in Leinster from hurt and all ill will."

"I thank you, Gracious Queen," Tristan said. "Now please tell me how you came to be riding in the wild hills where you found me. It seems to me a miracle that you should find me lying in a bog in this desolate country, especially as you must have known that the dragon lived there."

"It is a strange story. So listen carefully," the Queen said.

"The other evening a rumour reached the King's dun and whispered its way into the women's quarters. It was said that a certain steward, who purveys food and ale and other things for the King's household, had killed the dragon. My daughter and I know this steward well. He is a low-born and uncouth fellow, who is always leering at Isolt and desiring her with his eyes.

"Many years ago, when the King still hoped for a son to inherit his kingdom, he offered his daughter in marriage to any warrior who killed the Dragon of Wicklow. Since the steward began to desire Isolt, he has always followed behind any warrior who, he thought, intended to try to kill the dragon. He lacked the courage to face the beast when it was in full health and at full strength but he hoped to come on it when it had been wounded by some other, braver man and to finish it off. Then he would claim Isolt under the King's offer.

"When we heard that the steward claimed to have killed the dragon, Isolt threatened to kill herself, for she loathes the steward. But I told her that some other man must have killed the dragon because the steward would never have had the courage to do so.

"The steward's story was that he had seen an unknown warrior killed by the dragon and he said that the man and half his horse had been eaten by the beast but I suspected that the cowardly steward had only heard the dragon's death-cry and that he had then murdered and buried the unfortunate man who had killed it. We rode out early in the morning, hoping to find the man who had really killed the dragon, because we must disprove the steward's claim."

"I shall kill both the steward and myself, if he marries me," Isolt sobbed.

"No, no!" cried the Queen, embracing her daughter. "By fair means or foul we shall prevent it, whatever promises your father made long ago."

"Dear ladies!" Tristan said. "Do not let this steward distress you. I shall tell the King that it was I who killed the dragon."

"But the steward is showing everyone its head," Isolt wailed. "Your word is worth little against the dragon's head."

"If only you have brought the tongue which I had in my shirt or if you know where it is," Tristan said confidently, "I shall cry, 'checkmate!' to the steward's head."

"But the steward has said that he will bring twenty kinsmen to swear that they believe his word and he declares that, if anyone disputes it, he will prove his claim in single combat." Isolt objected.

"I might have difficulty in finding twenty friends to back my word" Tristan admitted. "But, when I am well again, I shall be willing to fight the steward."

"But you are a minstrel," Isolt protested.

"If a steward can fight," said Tristan, "then so can a minstrel. And, from what you tell me about this steward, I dare say that I am more courageous. Bring me my tongue and help me to regain my strength. Then you need fear neither the steward nor his claim," Tristan assured them.

The Queen showed Tristan the dragon's tongue, carefully wrapped up and locked in a box and she and Isolt did all that they could to bring Tristan back to his full strength. The Queen applied plasters, to draw out the poison left on his chest by the dragon's tongue and she dosed him with the "poison-herb" mashed in treacle, to drive out the fumes which he had breathed and she smeared with bullock's fat the many burns on his face and legs. Isolt meanwhile served him like a zealous squire.

When the claim was submitted, the King agreed to receive the steward in his court and he summoned his chiefs to assist him. But, before he went to the place of justice outside his hall, he came to ask his wife's advice, for she was not only skilled in healing but also very wise in matters of law.

"What do you advise, wife?" the King asked. "This matter weighs on me like death. It seems to me that I am bound to lose either my daughter or my honour, or both."

"Don't fret, My Lord. I can see a way to save both your daughter and your honour."

"Good! But tell me how, to set my mind at rest."

"Firstly, My Good Lord, the steward did not kill the dragon. Secondly, I know who did. Thirdly, I shall soon have proof positive of what I say. So go into your court with confidence and listen to what the steward has to say. Do not be afraid to admit that some years ago you offered to give your daughter to whoever killed the dragon but, when the moment comes to rebut the steward's claim, call upon me to speak for both of us and for Isolt."

When the King joined his chiefs upon the mound of justice, he found them all looking at the steward and discussing his good luck, but when the Queen brought Fair Isolt before the court, the chieftains saw that the steward and Isolt were an ill-assorted pair. "Like mating an angel with a pig!" they muttered in disgust.

The King cleared his throat and asked the steward: "What have you to say to me in the hearing of my chiefs?"

"Sire!" the steward crowed. "I demand that you honour your word given before witnesses. I require you to fulfil your undertaking to give your daughter, the Fair Lady Isolt, to any warrior who killed the dragon. Many brave men have died, while trying to win that rich prize, but because I loved the Lady, I have persevered in my untiring efforts to slay the terrible beast and at last through my great strength and boundless courage I have overcome it. After a desperate battle I killed the dragon. Therefore, Sire, make good your promise and give me the Lady Isolt."

The King was nettled by the steward's insolent speech but he followed his wife's advice and said quietly: "I have never yet gone back on my word, Master Steward; nor do I deny that I offered my daughter's hand to any warrior who killed the dragon."

Then the Queen stepped forward and spoke with haughty voice: "Sire, it is intolerable when a man claims a reward to which he has no right."

"But, Sire," the steward complained to the King, "it is for <u>you</u> to judge the case. Let me hear your answer to my demand."

"I shall require proof of the deed, before I award so rich a prize" the King replied sternly. "But it is not proper that I should both judge and plead my own case. Let the learned Queen speak for me and for herself and for the Lady Isolt."

"Master Steward!" said the Queen. "I do not doubt that your love is honest, nor that you deserve a good wife, but you ought not to aspire to the King's daughter on such a trumped-up claim."

"Trumped-up claim! What do you mean, Lady?" the steward cried angrily.

"I mean that you did not kill the dragon," the Queen answered sternly.

"But I have proof, Sire," the steward protested to the King and he signalled his servants to bring forward a cart. On the cart lay the dragon's head, horrid even in death. Its scaly neck had been sawn through by a carpenter and two men had been needed to lift the heavy head onto the cart.

"See! Here is my spear, thrust into the nostril, right through its mouth and out through its chops," the steward pointed. "By that means I was able to stop it breathing out flames and poisonous fumes, so that I could approach close enough to thrust my sword into its heart. And look at my sword, steeped to the hilt in the dragon's blood!"

"Anyone can get himself a bloody sword, when he finds a dead beast," the Queen argued. "And how can a lifeless head say <u>who</u>

killed it?" The Queen paused and addressed the King: "I have heard, Sire, that it was someone else who killed the dragon."

The lords sitting with the King whispered excitedly but the steward puffed out his chest. "I will swear on Saint Patrick's Blessed Staff and on any other holy relics that you like," he said. "And I have my twenty jurors who will swear that they believe me."

"Let us have no false oaths in this court, Sire!" pleaded the Queen and the twenty kinsmen whom the steward had brought to the court to back his oath looked doubtful and hung back. The steward's supporters whispered together and then advised the steward how to proceed.

"No one in the world, Sire," the steward declared, "would dare to tell me to my face and before this court that my claim is false, and if there is such a lying knave, I will prove my claim in arms."

The Queen in turn declared, "Sire, I undertake to produce before you in this court on the third day from now a man who will say that the steward's claim is false, and I confidently expect that either by argument or by oath or by arms he will prove that the steward is a liar."

The King consulted his advisers and then gave his ruling: "Provided that pledges are given for the appearance of both the steward and the Queen's champion in three days' time, I shall adjourn the court."

"I leave this jewelled ring in pledge that my champion will appear before you, ready, if necessary, to prove his argument in armed combat," the Queen declared, and she handed the King a ring from her finger.

"And here is <u>my</u> pledge that I shall be ready to prove my claim in combat," the steward cried and he pushed forward his younger brother to be the King's hostage until the day of trial.

CHAPTER 9

THE BROKEN BLADE

The Queen and the Lady Isolt did their best to bring Tristan back to his full strength and comeliness. In readiness for the expected combat against the steward who falsely claimed to have killed the dragon, the Queen's squire cleaned and polished Tristan's arms and armour.

Tristan's byrnie and helmet had originally been tinned, to prevent the iron rusting, but the blows of his many bitter battles had cut and cracked the protecting tin, and the scorching breath of the Wicklow Dragon had blistered it. Therefore the squire had to work carefully, in order to clean the rust from the iron without flaking off any more of the tin facing. He scoured the iron where that was exposed with pumice-stone and vinegar and polished the tin with brushes and cloths. He hung the armour up like laundry, the helmet on a peg and the byrnie stretched along a pole slung between two roof-beams. Tristan's splendid sword with its gilded hilt was in a sorry state, for the dragon's blood had corroded the iron blade. But the squire wrapped the blade in vinegary cloths and rubbed it with sand and finally he scoured it with pumice, until the dappled pattern of the hammered iron could be seen. When the blade was clean, he filed the edges to razorlike sharpness, lightly greased the iron and thrust the sword back into its handsome scabbard, which was made of wood, covered with wolf-skin and mounted with gold.

On the day before the trial in the King's court, Tristan was having a bath. Because the squire was busy scouring and cleaning Tristan's shield which had borne the brunt of the dragon's fiery and corrosive breath, Isolt had prepared Tristan's bath. Like a good squire, she had made sure that the water was the right heat and added healing herbs, and she had placed sponges for Tristan to sit on, so that he should not be pricked by splinters from the wooden bath-tub.

While Tristan was lying in the bath, Isolt sat on a chest waiting to wrap him in linen towels when he got out. She had often thought that Tristan had the upright bearing and the proud face of a nobleman and now, when she saw him naked, his straight limbs and rippling muscles seemed those of a warrior and an athlete rather than of a minstrel or a trader. That thought made her look at his armour and sword hanging on the wall.

It was a mystery to Isolt how a low-born minstrel had been able to kill a ferocious dragon which had defeated a thousand trained warriors, and now, as she examined Tristan's fine armour, she was even more puzzled.

What must it have cost, this byrnie? she wondered. Mail shirts were rare at that time and Tristan's was a work of art. Each tiny iron ring had been individually riveted and tinned and each was interlinked with six other rings. The iron shirt was strong but, everything considered, amazingly light and supple.

And this war-hat is that of a chieftain, Isolt said to herself. Tristan's helmet was a pointed dome made of four curved triangular iron plates riveted together and then strengthened by iron bands around the rim and covering the joins. That was the usual pattern for a helmet, although Irish helmets were rarely made of iron but Tristan's helmet not only had been tinned but also each rivet-head as well as the boar's head on the helmet's crest had been richly gilded.

The boar's head crest on top of Tristan's helmet reminded Isolt of something else which had puzzled her about this minstrel-trader. The splendid crest was cut and dented, as though it had been damaged in many battles and often repaired. The minstrel's right hand and his arms and legs were like that, too, for they were covered with a network of the neat, straight scars which a warrior gets in frequent sword-play.

That is another odd thing, Isolt thought. In Ireland only chiefs carried iron swords and they were usually short and broad-bladed. Ordinary men carried only spears and long knives. But this low-born merchant and harper had a most noble sword with a long iron blade and a gilded pommel and guard.

Isolt took the sword from its peg and drew the blade from its scabbard. She held the blade to the light, to see whether its surface had been badly damaged by the dragon's blood. She noticed the shimmering, dappled light on the blade caused by the way in which it had been made, for it had been hammered from a twisted rope of iron bars. She noticed also that a piece had been broken out of one of the edges.

Tantris may have damaged his sword on the dragon's scales, Isolt thought, but when she examined the gap, she could clearly see that the edge of the gap had been repeatedly filed together with the rest of the original edge of the blade. The damage was not recent.

The gap in the edge of Tristan's sword seemed vaguely familiar. Even before Isolt knew what it reminded her of, the shivers began to rise in waves from her feet; the skin on her cheeks grew taut over the bones; the hair on her scalp stood on end and cold sweat broke out on her body. It was as though her flesh guessed the horror to come, before her mind had grasped it. She glanced at Tristan lying dozing in his bath, and hurried frozen-faced from his hut carrying the sword to her mother's chamber.

Isolt opened a small box beside her mother's bed and took out the jagged piece of iron which her mother had found imbedded in the skull of her uncle Morolt. With trembling hands she fitted the fragment to the blade. Without any possible doubt this was the very sword which had killed her uncle two years previously. Her thumping heart was full of dread and her throbbing head was full of questions. *How did this vile sword come from Cornwall? How did Tantris get the sword with which Tristan murdered my uncle? Tantris! Tan! Tris! Tan! Tristan!* "Jesus God!" she cried, "Why did my head fail to understand the warning of my heart? That noble face! That strong body! Those battle-scars! That chieftain's armour! This kingly battle-blade!"

Tristan was still lying contentedly in his bath when Isolt came back like an avenging fury, and he was unaware of his danger, until she said to him, "So you are Tristan." The studied tonelessness of her voice warned him to take care and, without looking up, he answered casually, "No, Lady! I am Tantris."

"Tantris! Tristan! It is all the same, and whichever name you choose, you must die for the wrong which Tristan did me. With the sword by which Tristan killed my uncle, Tantris will die."

Then Tristan looked up. He saw Isolt standing over him with his sword raised high, but he showed no alarm and he spoke calmly. "In God's name, Lady, put that sword down. Even your reputation for beauty and charm could scarcely survive such an ugly deed as you now seem to be considering and that greasy, clumsy sword ill becomes your hands, the whitest and daintiest in all Ireland."

The Queen had seen Isolt run into Tristan's hut holding a naked sword and the tension of Isolt's figure, even seen from a distance, had warned the Queen that her daughter was in the grip of some savage emotion. She therefore hurried to Tristan's hut and entered, saying, "What is happening here? What are you doing, Isolt? Have you gone mad? Or are you playing a joke on Tantris? Why are you waving that huge sword? Do be careful. It has just been sharpened."

"Oh, Mother! This man is the murderer Tristan, who killed your brother. This is the man whom we are in duty bound to kill for vengeance," Isolt wailed.

"Is this Tristan? What makes you think so?" the Queen asked in disbelief.

"I am sure of it, Mother. The piece of iron which you took from Uncle Morolt's head fits this sword perfectly."

The Queen stared at Tristan. "If this youth is Tristan, my heart," she said, "has utterly deceived me." And it was clear that she did not believe it. But again Isolt raised the sword, crying: "Whether or not you believe it, Mother, I am going to kill him."

Tristan, still dripping, knelt in his bathtub and pressed his hands together palm to palm. "Mercy, Lovely Lady! Mercy!" he pleaded.

"Knave! Murderer! There is no mercy for you," Isolt cried but the sword wavered like grass in the wind.

"No, Isolt!" the Queen said firmly. "We cannot take vengeance upon this minstrel, for I have granted him my protection, so long as he is in Ireland."

"He cannot escape that way, Mother," Isolt argued. "You granted protection to Tantris but this is Tristan; and it is Tristan whom I am going to kill."

"Mercy, Isolt the Fair, Isolt the Bright Sun!" cried Tristan in his bath.

"Alas that ever I lived to see this day!" sobbed Isolt, dropping the sword and burying her face in her hands.

"Don't cry, dear. Don't cry," the Queen begged Isolt. "The grief of Morolt's death was more mine than yours, for I lost a brother and you only lost an uncle. But now my old grief seems small, because I am afraid of losing <u>you</u>. If you killed Tantris, who would be our champion against the hated steward?" she asked.

Tristan, who was still kneeling naked in his bath, thought it time to reason with the emotional ladies. "Dear Ladies!" he said. "It is true that in the past I have caused you distress but you ought not to forget that, to save his own life, a man must sometimes kill. Now, unless you prevent me, it is my hope to deal with the steward in a manner which will satisfy you and if you will put aside your dislike of me, I shall also tell you some very good news."

But at that the Queen threw up her hands and cried; "Now I know that you are indeed the hated murderer of my brother Morolt. I did not believe it, when Isolt told me but now I have heard it from your own mouth and my duty of revenge burns in my heart. Whatever promise I break, I must be true to Morolt and avenge his death."

The Queen seized the sword and raised it in both hands but Tristan cried: "Mercy, Gracious Queen!"

Just at that moment Bronwen walked in, and the amazed look on her face was so comical that Tristan began to smile. He was never in his life a merry-minded man but he saw the scene with the newcomer's eyes and he knew that it must be rather ridiculous. The two great ladies, the Queen and her daughter, stood with fierce eyes, tear-stained faces and wild, disordered hair and the Queen was brandishing a sword above her head, as though she were threshing corn with a flail. Before them knelt a man, like a felon saying his prayers before his head was cut off but he was stark naked and kneeling awkwardly in a puddle of dirty water in a bath-tub.

"What in heaven or earth is happening here?" Bronwen asked. "What are you doing?"

"Dear Cousin Bronwen!" wailed the Queen, lowering the sword and breaking into tears again. "Look at the viper whom we have been rearing for a nightingale. Look at the raven whom we have been feeding like a dove. Holy Jesus! We have twice nursed and healed our mortal foe, thinking him a friend. This is Tristan, Tristan of Cornwall, whom I have sworn to kill. Alas! What shall I do?"

"Whatever you do, Lady, do nothing hastily," Bronwen advised firmly and took the sword. "Certainly you cannot kill a man whom you yourself have promised to protect, especially as you have undertaken to produce him tomorrow before the King's court. My advice is that you let this man dress, while we discuss the matter outside."

While Tristan was dressing, Bronwen pointed out that there must be a very good reason for him to venture into the clutches of those who had sworn to kill him and the ladies decided to show him no ill will, until they had heard the good news of which he had spoken. Nevertheless, the Queen was embarrassed, when, on their return to Tristan's hut, he threw himself down on the floor at her feet, crying, "Mercy, Dear Ladies! Show me favour for the sake of my embassy."

The Queen found it hard to speak politely to him but Bronwen advised her, "My Lady, you must invite the Noble Lord to get up and you must at least honour your own word and promise him his life."

When Tristan had been allowed to get up, Bronwen asked for his news and he replied, "I have been sent here by the King of Cornwall to propose a marriage. King Mark offers his throne to the Lady Isolt and a bride-price of three hundred pennyweight of gold to King Angus."

For all that King Mark had been the mortal enemy of King Angus for many years, it was scarcely possible that Isolt would receive a better offer than this. In all the western world, no other reigning monarch was unmarried, and King Mark was rich enough and powerful enough to be able to preserve Isolt's Irish inheritance. The Queen could not afford to let sentiment stand in the way of a good bargain and she said at once: "If I had some guarantee of King

Mark's offer, I might support it. What is your opinion, cousin Bronwen?"

"I think that it would be an excellent match and I advise both of you to kiss the Noble Lord and to forget your ill will."

The Queen followed Bronwen's advice and at last Isolt also was persuaded to kiss Tristan but she was very reluctant.

"This proposal must be kept secret for the time being," Tristan warned the ladies. "Oh!" the Queen said, "I should like to tell My Lord, the King."

"Of course, Gracious Lady, the King must be told," Tristan agreed. "But remember that you have guaranteed my safety. I do not want to suffer, if he is angry."

The Queen sent the King a message that she had important news to tell him and the ladies waited in the women's hall. When the King arrived, the Queen knelt before him and asked a boon.

"I will refuse no reasonable request," the King assured her.

"My own Lord, the man who killed my brother Morolt is in my hands. Tristan, the King of Cornwall's heir, is here in your dun but I want you to grant him your favour and to forgive him all past ill will. He has come here on an important mission."

"Dear Lady, if you, who were Morolt's sister, can forgive Tristan, it would be wrong of me to carry on the feud, for I was related to Morolt only by marriage," the King replied, and when the Queen had told him Tristan's proposal of marriage between King Mark and Isolt, he nodded his head and said, "Good! I have been wondering how I could keep my word if Tantris' claimed Isolt for killing the dragon. I only hope that Tristan is authorised to make this proposal and to pay the bride-price."

When Tristan was brought in, he threw himself at the King's feet. "Mercy, Lord King!" he cried.

"Rise, Lord Tristan and come and kiss me. Since the ladies have renounced the feud, I also will make peace."

"Are my king and his lands and people included in this peace, Sire?" Tristan asked.

"Assuredly!" King Angus answered.

Then the King asked Tristan why he had come to Ireland, and when he had heard Tristan's story, he asked, "How can I be sure that your embassy from King Mark is genuine? Have you any proof of your authority to make this proposal and any guarantee of the terms of the marriage contract?"

"Certainly, Sire! I have brought with me twenty of the Cornish chiefs, and I believe that after the trial they will be able to pay you the bride-price, and to give you any assurances you want."

The King nodded and said, "Good!" Then he left them and went to his hall, to eat supper. But Tristan and the ladies laid their plans for the next day's trial, and Tristan sent a message to Master in his ship and gave him his orders.

CHAPTER 10

THE TRIAL

On the morning set for the trial of the steward's claim the open ground outside the fence of the mound of justice was crowded with sightseers. Some had been lured there by the fame of Isolt's beauty, and many had come hoping to see a battle, but most people had come simply to find out who was the Queen's champion, for no one had any idea.

The space within the fence, which was reserved for important people, was still nearly empty, when a splendid cavalcade rode up and the crowd goggled and whispered, "Who are these men? Have you ever seen forty men so richly clothed, and all with matching caps and cloaks? There are twenty chieftains wearing russet embroidered with gold, and twenty noble warriors wearing fine red cloaks interwoven with blue and edged with gold braid. And look! They have a noble escort of sixty archers with spears and also a learned master acting as their guide. Now the master is showing the ushers of the court a safe-conduct bearing the Queen's seal, and the twenty chieftains and twenty warriors are being led to places reserved for the nobility. Who can these noblemen be?'

The strangers took their places in dignified silence, and though they bowed politely to the Irish nobles standing near them, they spoke not a word. But a whisper in the crowd became a murmur and the murmur became a shout when some Cornish slaves recognised their kinsmen and childhood friends. The dignified silence of the noble strangers was cracked and broken open. They ran to the fence to call a greeting to this poor slave and to clasp the hand of that, and tears flowed freely.

"Holy Jesus! Cornishmen!" the crowd whispered and they wondered what would happen when King Angus discovered that his sworn enemies were in his court. However, when the King and his chiefs took their seats on the mound of justice, they bowed politely to the strangers and the crowd was mystified.

The steward and the twenty men who were to back his oath stood on one side before the King's bench, and the Queen and Isolt, glorious in face and figure and gorgeous in rich clothes and flashing jewels, were led to their places opposite the steward. As the two royal ladies walked into the court, the Queen murmured polite greetings, but the daughter bowed and flashed her smiling glance in silence and many people there thought it a shame to see such a paragon of beauty wasted on a boorish churl like the steward who had claimed her.

The steward was cock-a-hoop, for the ladies had brought no champion with them, and though he made enquiries, he heard no news of any champion. Therefore, he was confident as he stood before the King and said, "Sire, I am here to redeem my pledge and to restate my claim to the Lady Isolt. I have brought twenty jurors to back my claim and I am ready, if need be, to prove it in arms on anyone who disputes it. Where is the man who wished to deny me my rights? Has he got cold feet?"

The Queen stepped forward. Her gaze was mild, as she looked at the steward and her voice was friendly as she spoke. "For your own honour, good Master Steward, and by the honesty of the love which you say you have for my daughter, I ask you not to press your claim.

To be quite frank, Master Steward, the girl does not love you; indeed she hates you. In these circumstances it would be a kindness if you would drop your claim to marry her."

"Hah!" the steward exploded in scornful laughter. "Drop a claim which is not disputed? Abandon a case which I have already won? Forego the prize for which I have striven so long and hard and spent both sweat and blood? I have won your daughter, Lord King, and I mean to have her. If the Queen is unable to find the champion whom she pledged herself to produce in this court, then Sire, give judgment on my claim, for it is proven."

The King said sternly to the Queen, "You must produce your champion, Lady, or your case will go by default."

"Bring my man in," the Queen told her squire, and soon there was a stir among the crowd. Heads turned and tongues chattered. The gracious Lady Bronwen, younger cousin to the Queen and like an elder sister and an intimate adviser to the Fair Isolt, paced into the court. Perhaps she was unlucky to spend her life at the side of the Queen and Fair Isolt, whose beauty was dazzling, for she herself shared the family's good looks and she also was witty and accomplished. But even on this occasion, when she was not walking in the shadow of her more beautiful cousins, she was unlucky, for the crowd gaped not at her but at the tall man whom she led by the hand.

Tristan had told Master to send his clothes-chest from the ship to the Queen's quarters and before the trial he had dressed with the greatest care in his richest clothes. On his head he wore a gold circlet encrusted with pearls and jewels, and the vast cloak which he wore over his shining byrnie was of dark red silk, heavily embroidered with gold thread and over-sewn with a network of pearls. Behind him walked the Queen's squire, carrying his shining helmet and glowing shield, his sharp-edged spear and gilded sword.

"Wah! What a champion! This is a prince, no less," the crowd whispered and the King and Queen proved his quality by rising to receive him. But the Cornish chiefs and Tristan's warrior-companions, who had stood until now in silent dignity, shouted and cheered and crowded round their leader, and they escorted Bronwen and Tristan to their places beside the Queen and Isolt. Tristan bent the knee and bowed low to the King, the Queen and Fair Isolt, and when silence had been commanded, he announced, "I am the Queen's champion in this cause. What does the steward claim?"

The steward was daunted by the noble appearance of the Queen's champion and the quality of his arms but he declared manfully, "Sir, whoever you are, I claim that I slew the Dragon of Wicklow and I claim the hand of the King's daughter, which was the prize offered by the King in the presence of his chiefs and great men."

"Sir, whatever you claim, you did not slay the dragon," Tristan answered calmly.

"I did and I can prove it."

"What is your proof?"

"This head, Sir!" shouted the steward and he pointed to the cart with the dragon's head.

"That beast's tongue will never bear witness to support your claim," Tristan said scornfully but the steward seized his chance.

"Sire! Sire!" he cried. "Command your men to open the dragon's jaws. They will find its tongue skewered on my spear, for, as you can see, my spear goes right through the dragon's mouth from top to bottom."

"Lord King!" said Tristan, "I agree that the dragon's tongue should decide the matter. If the beast's tongue is found to be skewered on the steward's spear, I shall give him best and withdraw my opposition.

The King told his ushers to open the dragon's jaws and the crowd craned their necks, trying to see inside the large mouth. Those who stood nearest looked at one another in astonishment. They could see plenty of terrifying teeth and also the wooden shaft of the steward's spear, but there was certainly no tongue anywhere in the mouth.

"It must have been a tongueless dragon," cried the steward.

"No!" Tristan said. "<u>This</u> is the dragon's tongue." And he took a box from Bronwen's hands and showed the tongue to the King and the chiefs sitting on the King's bench. They nodded their heads and began to laugh and one of them got up and put the tongue into the dragon's mouth, to see that the tongue fitted its root.

"I think that it is clear, Lord King, that this tongue could not have been removed while the dragon was alive," Tristan pointed out. "And it is also clear that, if there had been a tongue in the dragon's mouth when the steward thrust his spear through the jaws, the spear would have transfixed the tongue. It follows, therefore, that the dragon was already dead when the steward so bravely attacked it."

Amid increasing laughter the steward shouted shrilly, "The dragon's tongue has been stolen from me. I will swear an oath on any sacred relics that you like, and I have here behind me twenty good men who will swear that they believe me." But his friends refused to back his oath, whatever he swore.

"Lord King!" said Tristan, "if your men search deeper inside the dragon's mouth, I believe they will find another spearhead, for, when I met the dragon, with my first thrust I buried my spear-blade deep in its gullet."

"I demand to prove my claim and to defend my honour in combat, Sire!" the steward shouted wildly, but his brother told him that it would be foolish to throw away his life as well as his honour.

"What chance have you against the man who killed the

dragon?" the young man said. "And, besides, just take a look at that strong and supple body and those well-made arms." In the end the steward was pushed onto his knees by his friends and, stuttering and stammering and looking very small, he withdrew his claim to the Lady Isolt.

"Ha, steward!" the Queen cried scornfully. "I never expected you to abandon a case which you had already won, nor to forego a prize which you had earned with such sweat and blood. Count yourself lucky that you still <u>have</u> some blood."

With jeers and blows, with kicks and curses, the steward was chased from the King's court and his kinsmen and friends gave him no help, for they were deeply ashamed of him. Tristan, however, stood before the King and in a ringing voice declared, "Sire, I claim the prize for killing the dragon. I claim the Lady Isolt."

"I grant you the prize, Noble Lord, in the terms of your proposal to me," the King replied. Then the King announced to his chiefs and people that King Mark of Cornwall had sent his heir and his chiefs to offer marriage to the Lady Isolt; he announced that peace had been made between Morolt's kinsmen and Tristan and between the people of Leinster and the people of Cornwall. He announced that he was willing to bind the peace firmly by marrying his daughter to King Mark. Then Tristan and the Cornish chiefs swore that Isolt should be Queen of Cornwall and that her children by King Mark should be first heirs to the Kingdom of Cornwall. Piece by piece they weighed out and paid the bride-price of 300 pennyweight of gold. Finally King Angus put Isolt's hand into that of Tristan, in token that he handed her over to King Mark's ambassador.

"Sire!" Tristan said. "On behalf of my Lord, King Mark, and of my Lady, Isolt the Queen-to-be, I ask a boon. I ask you to give into my Lady's charge all those Cornish noblemen who were enslaved because of the tribute which used to be paid."

"Certainly, Lord Tristan!" said the King. "They shall all go home with you."

So the noble Cornish slaves were set free. Their former masters gave them good clothes and they were entertained as the King's guests until the day of departure.

"Tristan has the Devil's own luck," the Cornish chiefs grumbled. But, though they begrudged him his success, they showed him friendly and respectful faces. In spite of their jealousy, Tristan had pleased them by winning a bride for King Mark, for, on the assumption that this healthy girl would give the King a handful of strong sons, Tristan had barred himself from inheriting the Kingdom of Cornwall. He, on the other hand, did not mind that at all, for he had had both an exciting adventure and a spectacular triumph; he had won the best bride in all Christendom for his dear Lord and at last he was popular with his fellow-courtiers.

50 FOOT TRADING SHIP OF 800 A.D.

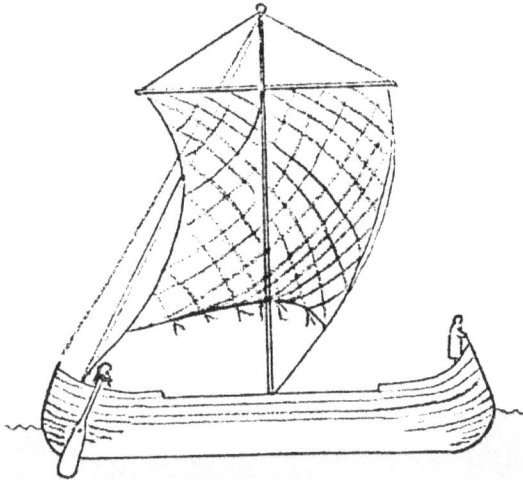

CHAPTER 11

THE LOVING CUP

Since the King of Leinster had betrothed his daughter to the King of Cornwall, preparations were made for her departure.

Tristan hired three more ships to carry the freed Cornish slaves back to Cornwall, and he hired an especially large and handsome Frisian ship to carry the Fair Isolt and her ladies. The seamen cleaned the small triangle of deck beneath the quarterdeck where the steersman stood in the stern of the Frisian ship; the dark cavern was hung with embroidered cloths to make a cabin for the princess and a tent of canvas was rigged up against the entrance to Isolt's cabin for her ladies in waiting and female slaves. There would be no other men in the ladies' ship except Tristan himself, his Master serving him and the Frisian sailors; but the ladies' ship would be escorted by the six other ships as protection against sea-robbers.

Tristan and the Cornishmen were lodged and feasted in the King's dun as his honoured guests, and the King assembled four pairs of Irish hounds, four matched Irish stallions and a richly-decorated four-horse chariot as a gift for King Mark. But the busiest place was within the fence of the Queen's quarters, for the women had to make ready Isolt's baggage.

A bride must take with her all that she would need except the house, furniture and food, which her husband must provide, so Isolt's belongings filled ten large oak chests. The women made new clothes of linen, cloth, silk and fur, and they embroidered linen to hang around Isolt's bed and on her walls. They packed tablecloths, knives and spoons, cups and serving-dishes, pots and pans and spits; they packed herbs, spices and medicines, because the lady of the house was also its doctor. They packed her gear for spinning and weaving, her musical instruments and her books.

The Queen and her cousin Bronwen chose ten young ladies of good birth and ten female slaves to serve Isolt both on the voyage, and in her new home. The Queen asked Bronwen herself to be Isolt's chaperone, the guardian of her honour, and her close counsellor. Bronwen was reluctant to leave her homeland and her friends, but both the Queen and Isolt said that only if Bronwen went with Isolt, could mother and daughter bear the parting. Often the sorrowful Queen gave Bronwen instructions for her daughter's guidance, and she told Bronwen that she would hold her entirely responsible both for Isolt's honour and for her happiness.

The great day came when Ireland's Flower, the Fair Isolt, must sail away to her wedding in Cornwall. A long procession wound its way from the King's dun to Tristan's ships. First, the freed slaves went aboard, then Tristan's warrior-band, and then the Cornish chiefs. The Cornishmen were smiling and happy to be going home. But behind them, where Tristan led the Fair Isolt's horse, both Isolt and her women were wailing loudly. The King, the Queen and all those who had come to do their princess honour wept to see her go, for in those days women rarely crossed the sea so it was very unlikely that Isolt and her women would ever come back.

At last the kissing was done and the farewells had been said. Tristan led his Queen-to-be up the plank and into the ship. The seamen strained and heaved to push their ship off the shelving shore. With ten strokes of the oars they gave the captain steerage way and he ordered them to hoist the square sail. The large limp sail swelled with the breeze; the hull's tarred timbers quivered with life and the travellers lifted their voices in an ancient hymn, praying for a fair wind and protection from both storms and robbers.

"God bless you!" King Angus shouted.

"God keep you safe!" answered Tristan.

Isolt, standing at Tristan's side, sobbed and drooped on Bronwen's shoulder. Tristan patted her arm and tried to console her but she shrugged him off and turned her back on him, so Bronwen led her away to her cabin. Tristan, however, stood by the stern-post and gazed astern until Dublin was only a smudge of grey huts in the distance. Then he told the captain to set course for the Welsh coast and he stationed his other ships to windward of his own ship, so that they could at once run down-wind to help if any trouble threatened.

Tristan and Master guarded the entrance to the ladies' tent and they were always armed, for Tristan wanted to prevent the sailors from stealing Isolt's belongings or embarrassing her women. Isolt's cabin in the stern could be entered only by passing through the tent where her twenty women lived, outside of which Tristan and Master stood guard. No man ever entered the ladies' tent except Tristan himself, who was in charge of his uncle's bride-to-be.

Even after an hour's rest Isolt was still crying for her homeland, and when Tristan went to pay his respects, he tried to comfort her. He put his arm around her shoulders and said, "Don't cry, Lady."

But Isolt pushed him away, saying spitefully, "I hate you."

"By the host of Heaven, why, Gracious Lady?"

"Because . . . you killed my uncle Morolt."

"But that feud has been set aside. You yourself gave me the kiss of peace on that quarrel."

"Then I hate you for taking me away from my family and my home, and for carrying me off to an unknown husband in an unknown land."

"Lady, you are growing in honour with every mile that you travel from your old nursery to your new throne. For the King of Cornwall is a sovereign who owes no one allegiance and you will be his crowned Queen with power and riches and honour such as you never had in Ireland."

"Believe me, Lord Tristan, I would rather be poor but happy than rich and miserable"

"Yes, Lady! I agree with you in that. But in Cornwall you will be both rich and happy; whereas, if I had not come to your rescue, you might by now have been married to the loathly steward and then, I believe, you would have been not only poor, but miserable as well."

"It will be a long time before I thank you for anything, Lord Tristan. If I had married that man, I should have reformed him," Isolt boasted. "And I should have been in my own homeland still and among my own people."

"With respect, Gracious Lady, Fair Isolt, you could never have made a silk purse out of that sow's ear. But I am taking you to a king who is brave, kind, noble and rich and your life will be both happy and honourable."

Isolt fell silent but she would not speak graciously to Tristan. She still disliked him both for her uncle's sake and for her own.

When the ship drew away from the coast and met the full force of the wind and the ocean swell, the ladies began to feel seasick. They had never before been in unsheltered waters and they felt so ill that they thought that they were going to die. One after another they ran from their tent to vomit. Tristan and Master were kept busy all night, guiding them to the leeward side of the heaving ship and supporting them, so that they did not fall overboard.

Early in the morning the forward lookout shouted, "Land ho! Land ho!" The captain told Tristan that their landfall was at Holyhead on Anglesey.

"The ladies need a rest, after such a night, Captain. Put into a sheltered bay, so that they can go ashore and stretch their legs," Tristan ordered.

The captain put into a bay and Isolt's women were rowed ashore, to play on the sands under the watchful eyes of Master who was armed, and Bronwen. No other men were allowed to land, for fear that they might molest the women, and Tristan would not let Isolt go ashore, for fear of an accident.

Tristan put his oak chest against the ship's side on the open deck and draped his cloak over the gunwale, so that Isolt could sit in the fresh air. He himself sat on the deck at her feet, to keep her company and to distract her thoughts from homesickness and seasickness. He played the harp and then he sang. But, whenever he tried to pat her hand, she avoided his touch if she possibly could, saying angrily, "Let me alone, Lord Tristan"

Towards midday Tristan became thirsty, for the hot May sun was reflected from the sea and the pinewood deck; there was no breeze in the sheltered bay. Isolt asked a little serving-maid to bring a cup of wine. The maid searched in the cabin and brought back a wooden drinking-bowl and a small flask of wine.

"I found this bottle among the belongings of the Lady Bronwen," she said.

"I am sure that Bronwen would not mind us helping ourselves in our great need," said Isolt and she told the maid to pour a cup of wine for Tristan.

Tristan sipped the wine and licked his lips. "This wine is sweet and mellow but strong and fiery too. It is as soft as swan's down but as sharp as a well-filed sword," he said and took a gulp to wet his dry throat. "Gracious Lady, drink some of this wine, I beg you. It will help you to forget your troubles and it will bring the roses back to your ivory cheeks."

Tristan handed the bowl to Isolt. She was reluctant to share a cup with the man who had killed her uncle and who had taken her from her family but she was thirsty and she thought that strong wine was a medicine which might cure her sea-sickness. Therefore she took the cup and raised it to her lips. First she sipped, and then she swallowed the wine and it warmed her to the heart.

Even as Isolt had put out her hands to take the cup, Tristan noticed the pale elegance of her long, slim fingers and, when her head was tilted back to drink, he noticed the delicacy of her skin, and the veins showing blue on the marble column of her neck. He noticed her hard young breasts pressing proudly against the linen of her summer smock; he noticed the smallness of her waist, where her smock was girdled with a cord and he noticed the smooth, rounded surface of her thighs where the smock was stretched over them and fell into the deep and modest valley of her lap.

Tristan's breathing stopped; his whole body trembled and he drew a deep, shuddering breath and let it go in a gasp. He felt as though his eyes were standing out on stalks and, lest his eyes should betray his unruly thoughts, he looked quickly down at Isolt's feet, which peeped from the hem of her smock like two timid black mice. When she handed the cup back to him, he buried his flushed face in its depths without a word of thanks and slowly drained it to the dregs.

Isolt looked at Tristan, as though she saw him for the first time. She gazed at his bronzed skin, his short brown beard and the muscled tree-trunk of his neck; she studied the strong, scarred hand which gripped the cup, the hairy forearm, the broad, firm shoulders, the deep chest, small waist, massive thighs and calves, the narrow knees and slender ankles. When he lowered the cup and thus unsheathed the steel-blue swords of his eyes, she hid her confusion by staring at his feet in their broad leather shoes.

The little maid refilled the bowl and Isolt and Tristan drank and drank again. No longer was Isolt reluctant to share a cup with Tristan; indeed she tried to touch his hand as they passed the cup to and fro. But Tristan was uneasy. He no longer tried to pat her hand or to put his arm around her shoulders in kindly fashion and he did not dare to look her in the face, for fear that his staring eyes might reveal the madness of his mind.

Tristan felt utterly bewildered and his head was spinning. His heart reached out to Isolt's heart; his eyes craved to tangle with her eyes and his body yearned for her body. But Isolt was both one king's daughter and another king's bride, and she had been entrusted to his care as the loyal ambassador between them. His mind told him that, if he offended those two powerful kings, he would be in danger wherever he went, and his soul told him that if he betrayed his trust, his honour would be gone forever.

Isolt also was perplexed, when she found that her dislike of Tristan had turned to liking, indeed to more than liking - love; but she was not troubled by any thoughts of danger or dishonour. She was valuable goods being traded to obtain an alliance but she knew that her doting father would never hurt her, and as she herself had not been consulted about the marriage, she did not feel that her honour was engaged to be faithful to King Mark. She was perplexed simply because she was young and inexperienced. She loved Tristan and she wanted nothing more than to love him, and to be loved by him. But she had no idea whether he loved her and she did not know how to find out.

Tristan and Isolt sat tongue-tied and they avoided each other's eyes. Whenever they tried to make conversation, they both spoke at once. Then they were abashed into silence once again. Whenever they tried to feed their hungry love with their eyes, their glances crossed and they looked away in embarrassment. Their precious moments alone together wasted away in doubt and discomfort, until the shore party returned to the ship. Then their tongues were loosened and Isolt told Bronwen, "Please forgive us, Cousin. We became so thirsty that we drank your little bottle of wine."

Bronwen shrank back, as though her face had been slapped and she whispered, "What? You and Tristan?"

"Yes!" answered Isolt.

"Alas! My honour has gone overboard," Bronwen cried. "And you two will die for your theft."

"You are talking unseemly nonsense, Bronwen," Isolt said sternly. "You had better lie down in case you have got a touch of sunstroke."

Bronwen buried her face in her hands and turned sadly away. But after that she kept a constant watch on Tristan and Isolt, which embarrassed them still more.

The ships weighed anchor and put out to sea again but Tristan and Isolt were tormented by their love. Each fought the enemy within their hearts. Tristan's sense of loyalty and honour forbade him to speak of love to his uncle's bride-to-be and Isolt's modesty silenced her. But their inner struggles were revealed by their cheeks, which blushed and went pale by turns, and by the sighs which escaped their lips. For that reason, although they struggled against the trap which held them tightly, and although they spoke not a single word of love, each began to guess that the other was similarly afflicted.

One day they were sitting in Isolt's small cabin, and although Bronwen was with them, Isolt broached the subject which was in her heart. "Lord Tristan," she said, "do you remember how, when we first met, I gladly learnt everything that you chose to teach me?"

"Yes, My Lady! You were an eager pupil."

"I should be an eager pupil now, Lord Tristan, if you wished to teach me any other noble art. Particularly so, if you would teach me what I most want to know!"

"Indeed, Lady! What is that?"

But Isolt was too shy to ask him to teach her about love. Instead she reminded him how on two occasions she had recognised him—when she had found him lying unconscious in a bog and again when she had seen him lying naked in a bath.

"Ah!" she whispered. "If I had known then what I know now, I should certainly have killed you."

"What do you mean, Gracious Lady?" Tristan asked in surprise.

"If I had known then that you would cause me such pain and grief, Lord Tristan, I should not have let you live to torment me like this."

"But, Lovely Lady, not for all the world would I willingly cause you either pain or grief. What is this torment of which you complain and which you say is caused by me?"

"It is a very sharp pain, My Lord, and I feel it all the time, like a knife turning in my body." Isolt paused and took Tristan's hand. "I will show you where my pain is," she said, and she carried his hand to her left breast and pressed it against her heart. "That is where you have hurt me and I do not know how to cure it."

"Lady, I have a pain in just the same place," Tristan whispered. "See! Here it is," he said and held her hand close against his chest. "Fair Isolt, bright sun not only of Ireland but of the whole world, you have robbed me both of my reason and of my honour. I can think of nothing except you and your enchanting beauty."

"Lord Tristan, it is the same with me. The world is empty except for you," Isolt whispered back.

Tristan was able to delay their voyage south along the coast of Wales by using as an excuse the ladies' seasickness and the rough weather. The ladies went ashore at several places but Bronwen always stayed beside the lovers and although they held hands and whispered secrets and sometimes stole a kiss, they pined away to skin and bones. They ate nothing. They were dying of love.

Bronwen carefully observed Tristan and Isolt. She noticed their loving glances, their blushes, sighs and accidentally-on-purpose touching of hands. She saw that they could not eat and she realised that they were so lovesick that they really might die. She decided to help them. "What is the matter, you two ghosts?" she asked. "Stop moping and tell me your troubles."

Tristan sighed. "We dare not tell you, Lady Bronwen," he said, "unless you promise to keep our secret to yourself."

"I give you my word on that, and I offer my help too," Bronwen said encouragingly.

"Dear Lady, we are dying of love," Tristan whispered. "And since the day when we offended you by taking your wine, you have not once left us alone together. Help us to meet, Bronwen or we shall soon be dead."

"Is this the truth, My Lady?" Bronwen asked sternly. "Are you as lovesick as the Lord Tristan says?"

Isolt sighed, as though her heart would break. "Yes, dear Cousin!" she answered.

"How the Devil mocks us!" Bronwen cried bitterly.

Then she added firmly: "Even if it brings me to sorrow and you to shame, I will do what you want. Do not, for my sake, refrain from anything which your health requires, but for your own sakes try to master your passion and do nothing which the world would think shameful, unless really and truly you cannot help it. Lady Isolt, your mother gave your honour into my custody. Now I give it into your own custody. Do what you like with it but please be careful; or you may lose not only your honour but your life as well."

That night, when the ship was shrouded in darkness, Tristan left his place outside the ladies' tent. He crept through the tent, stepping carefully over the sleeping women, towards Isold's cabin. He pushed aside the curtain which covered the entrance and he felt with his hands, until he found Bronwen's shoulder, for Bronwen always slept in Isolt's bed, lying between her and possible danger. Gently Tristan shook her until Bronwen awoke and then he reached across to touch Isolt's face reassuringly. Isolt seized his hand and covered it with kisses and, when Bronwen asked, "Shall I go, My Lady?" Isolt answered fiercely, "Yes! Go quickly and let My Lord come in to me."

With a grief-stricken sob, Bronwen slipped from the bed and crept away into the tent beyond the curtain and Tristan took her place beside Isolt. All the night long, while Tristan and Isolt were locked in love, Bronwen kept watch outside the cabin and, when the pallid dawn separated the dark sky from the dark sea, she reached in and shook Tristan's foot and warned him to go back to his place. In the morning they were a weary-looking trio but Tristan and Isolt had roses in their cheeks, for love had cured their lovesickness.

Tristan and Isolt were enraptured. They thought they were at the gates of Heaven but the lookout called, "Land ho! Land ho!" And the Cornish travellers cried joyfully, "It is Lundy Island and we are nearly home." Soon the happy Cornishmen were pointing out: "Cornwall! Cornwall!" And, before the sun had set, they were dancing merrily on the decks and shouting, "Tintagel! There is Tintagel!"

In a few short hours Tristan and Isolt fell from Heaven to Hell, for to them it would have been Heaven to sail the sea forever in each other's arms, and it seemed like Hell to be brought so soon to King Mark's presence.

A CELTIC CHURCH

CHAPTER 12

BRONWEN'S PRICE

When Tristan's fleet was sighted from Tintagel, King Mark was out hunting. Isolt had to wait for a long time, swinging at anchor in Tintagel Haven, before the King came aboard to welcome her. She saw the King's palace nestling in a valley, but the treeless cliffs and frowning headlands which towered around her showed that this was a harsher country than her native Leinster. She felt homesick, frightened and lonely, for, although Tristan held her hand, she knew that he meant to deliver her like trade goods to his uncle and she dreaded her unknown husband as though he were an ogre.

However, when King Mark came down to meet his bride, he was as friendly and thoughtful as could be. He praised her beauty and complimented her on the few Cornish words which she had learnt. He asked after her health and advised her to rest in the women's quarters until she had recovered from the voyage.

Best of all, he put her unreservedly into the charge of Tristan. "For," he said to Tristan in her hearing, "you won my bride and arranged the marriage and you have brought her safely across the sea to me. Therefore you shall have full charge of her until the wedding."

While the King sent out his messengers to summon his chiefs and all the great men to his wedding, Tristan and Isolt were always in each other's company, and whenever they were alone together or even when Bronwen was with them, they behaved unashamedly like lovers. They seized their chances like men condemned to die, for they did not know what would happen when Isolt was married to King Mark. As the fateful day came closer, they made love more passionately so that on her wedding day, in spite of her anxiety, Isolt glowed like the midday sun.

The Cornish chiefs gasped and shaded their eyes before such proud and radiant beauty and they repeated Tristan's verse: "Isolt the Fair, Isolt the Sun, her beauty dazzles everyone. Isolt the Sun, Isolt the Fair, sheds golden glory everywhere."

Saint Materiana's Church, high on the downs above the palace, was very small, so King Mark and Isolt were married at its door while all the great men of the kingdom of Cornwall stood in the churchyard. The royal wedding was celebrated in the sight of all, so that there could be no argument about it. Tristan, as the matchmaker, formally gave Isolt away by placing her hand in King Mark's and the bridal couple exchanged rings, shared a cup of wine and were blessed as one, to impress the wedding on the witnesses' memory.

After the ceremony King Mark and his bride were led down a flower-strewn path to the King's hall. First King Mark took his seat on the dais and then Tristan led Isolt forward to sit beside the King. The King himself placed the Queen's crown upon Isolt's head and all the great men did homage, bending the knee before her and shouting, "Hail, Fair Isolt, Queen of Cornwall!"

The King declared that Isolt of Leinster was now Isolt of Cornwall, with all the privileges of the Queen of Cornwall and he announced that her children would be his rightful heirs and that Tristan would inherit Cornwall only after Isolt's children and their issue. At that the Cornish chiefs smiled in their beards, because their plan to oust Tristan from the inheritance seemed at last to have succeeded, but they could not help saying spitefully, "That peacock Tristan has the Devil's own luck. Fancy bringing off an Irish marriage for the King of Cornwall. Two months ago we all thought that it was impossible."

After the wedding and the Queen's installation came the wedding feast during which the wine flowed freely. But at last there arrived the moment which Tristan, Isolt and Bronwen had been dreading. The feast was becoming rowdy and the King was beginning to get drunk. It was time for the bride to retire to bed.

Isolt did not want to go to bed with King Mark. This was not because she disliked him, for he was honourable, generous and kind. But she was utterly in love with Tristan and she belonged to Tristan body and soul.

Tristan's flesh crept at the thought of Isolt's ordeal. But at the same time he was both deeply ashamed of deceiving his uncle and yet, also unreasonably jealous.

Bronwen, who from childhood had been close to Isolt, felt with her own heart and with her own body how unpleasant for Isolt this night would be and she felt sick.

But the three conspirators felt not only distaste but also fear. They dreaded what would happen when King Mark found that his little bride was not a virgin, for, if the truth came out, they all expected to be tortured to death in a most shameful and painful manner. It was this fear which the three discussed when Tristan and Bronwen led Isolt to the King's sleeping-hut to await her bridegroom.

"There is only one solution" Isolt said at last. "Bronwen, who is a virgin, must take my place in the King's bed."

"Yes!" Tristan agreed. "The King was already rather drunk, when we left the hall and I will make sure that he is really fuddled, before he comes to bed. If we put out most of the lamps and shade the others, he will be unable to see Bronwen properly and he will not notice the difference."

"How the Devil mocks us!" Bronwen cried in anguish, but she did not refuse the distasteful task which Tristan and Isolt were forcing upon her. "My honour went overboard, when you took my wine," she said sadly. "And this is the price which I must pay for my carelessness."

"What are you talking about? Isolt asked suspiciously.

"Dear Lady, your mother entrusted me with the custody of your honour and happiness but because of my laziness you have lost them both" Bronwen explained. "When you and Tristan drank my flask of wine, you drank poison, for that flask held a powerful love-potion, which your mother had told me to give to you and your husband on your wedding-night. When you and Tristan shared that loving-cup, you drank your death"

"For such a death, I would drink your poison every day," cried Tristan. "Isolt my life, Isolt my death, I speak your name with every breath. Isolt my death Isolt my life, if you are death, then death's my wife."

Tristan and Isolt were delighted to hear that they had been locked in lifelong love by the Queen of Leinster's love-potion, but Bronwen realised that their unlawful love would bring unhappiness, dishonour and death to them and perhaps to her as well.

"It is because I failed to guard the Queen's love-potion that you two lovers are in this difficulty and therefore it is my duty to rescue you from your present danger," Bronwen said. "But the Devil has tricked us completely and in the end, we shall not escape."

Isolt laid Bronwen naked in the King's bed and dressed herself in Bronwen's clothes. Then Tristan put out all the lamps and left only one candle to give a little light and he fetched King Mark from the hall. The conspirators were lucky. The King was full of wine and rather unsteady and, when Tristan undressed him, he rolled happily into bed without noticing that the warm young woman lying beside him was not Isolt.

Tristan and Isolt stood anxiously in the shadows but, as time went by without any angry commotion from the bridal bed, they breathed more easily. The King had not noticed, and the lovers were safe for the time being. But Isolt in her relief turned her fears quite upside down and imagined that Bronwen was trying to supplant her as Queen of Cornwall. She remembered that persuading Bronwen to take her place in the King's bed had been surprisingly easy and she imagined that Bronwen was spilling the terrible truth into King Mark's ear. Isolt crept to the bed and listened for the tell-tale whispering that she feared but she heard nothing except the King's heavy and ever heavier breathing.

As soon as the King began to snore, Bronwen slipped out of bed and Isolt's feelings did another somersault. Tenderly she embraced her unfortunate cousin and squeezed her hand in sincere gratitude, before she herself lay down beside the King. Because the King had drunk so much, he soon got up to relieve himself and Tristan, with a candle, lighted him back to bed and handed him a loving-cup of wine to share with his newly bedded bride. The King did not notice the change in his bed-companion; he spoke to Isolt courteously and kindly and he shared with her his cup of wine, as tradition required when a man had just taken a lady's maidenhead.

For the rest of that night Tristan and Bronwen squatted together in a corner of the King's bedroom. At first Tristan put his arm around Bronwen, to comfort her, for she was shivering after her unpleasant ordeal. But soon it was Bronwen who had to soothe Tristan, for, when the bed creaked, the pangs of jealousy pierced his heart and disgust choked him.

"Did I not tell you that you drank your death with that love-potion, Lord Tristan?" Bronwen whispered.

"This is not death. It is dishonour," Tristan answered. "For I must bear this every day, and no one can die daily."

The lovers had avoided their first difficulty and they settled down to a bitter-sweet life in King Mark's palace. Tristan was trusted by the King and he could enter the Queen's quarters whenever he liked. He and Isolt could be together often but both of them were at King Mark's command and they had to serve him, the one as squire and the other as wife. As always happens, Tristan and Isolt were coarsened by their life of lies. Tristan served King Mark more for the purpose of deceiving him with his wife than for the sake of their long and loyal companionship, and Isolt was always on the watch for anything which might threaten her freedom to be with Tristan. In particular, Isolt began once more to suspect Bronwen. No one except Bronwen knew the lovers' secret and Isolt still feared that Bronwen, having taken her place in the King's bed on the bridal night, might hope to win the King for herself by betraying the lovers.

Isolt spoke to two slaves who did heavy work around the palace, two English warriors who had been captured in a border scuffle. She told them that they could earn their freedom and a piece of gold to pay their way home, if they would kill someone who had wronged her. Of course they agreed but they were dismayed, when they saw whom she wanted them to murder.

"I am sickening for a fever, cousin," Isolt told Bronwen. "Please go to the forest and fetch me the plant called Fever-few, so that I can make myself some medicine. These two men will give you escort, for they know where the plant is to be found."

The two slaves led Bronwen deep into the forest, far from any house. Then they dismounted and lifted her from her horse. One man held her arms, and the other drew his long knife.

"Mercy, masters! Mercy!" Bronwen cried in terror. "What are you going to do?"

"We were told to kill you. The Queen herself gave us the order. What great wrong have you done her?"

"Hold your hand, while I answer," Bronwen said, "and tell My Lady exactly what I say, when you return to her. I never did her any wrong but once and this is what happened. When the Lady Isolt and I left our home, each of us packed a clean white smock, but during the voyage My Lady became so heated that she wore her smock both night and day. When we reached Tintagel, My Lady's smock was torn and dirty and she could not wear it for her wedding. She asked me to give her my smock which I had kept clean. Alas! Perhaps My Lady thought that I was reluctant to give her my clean smock on her wedding-night. If that is not the reason why she desires my death, I can think of no other, for I have always served her faithfully and I have always worked for her good rather than my own.

"Good masters, greet My Lady from me and tell her that I forgive her my death and ask God to have her in His keeping, as I trust that He now has me."

The two slaves were confused. They knew that the Lady Bronwen had been the Queen's friend and they doubted that she had ever done anything deserving death. They were afraid of making a mistake and they decided to go back to Isolt to make sure of her orders. So they lifted Bronwen into the fork of a tree and tied her there, so that she should be safe from wild beasts but unable to escape and they rode back to Tintagel.

The two slaves told Isolt that they had carried out her orders and they told her what Bronwen had said. Their words took Isolt by the throat and choked her with guilt and remorse. "God have mercy! What have you done?" she screamed at the two men. "Murderers! Cut-throats! I will have you hanged."

"The gods preserve us, Lady!" The slaves protested. "It was you who told us to kill the poor girl. We undertook to do it only because you offered us our freedom. But, if it is a matter of our life or hers, you shall have her back. We will go and fetch her."

"Don't try to deceive me," Isolt shouted. "One of you must stay here, while the other goes into the forest and, if the one who goes does not come back, the one who is in my power will die most horribly. But, if you bring back my friend safe and sound, you shall have the freedom and the gold which I promised you"

When Bronwen was brought back to the palace, Isolt received her with tears and kisses. She freed the slaves and sent them out of Cornwall, to keep them quiet, but she told Bronwen that her murder plot had only been a game to test her loyalty and she swore that she would never again either doubt or test her. Although Isolt's excuse was untrue, her promise to trust Bronwen in future was kept faithfully and she trusted her thereafter.

The King and Queen were always in the company of their close counsellors, Tristan and Bronwen, and each of the four treated the others loyally and generously, although three of them shared some guilty secrets. Even the unlawful love of Tristan and Isolt began to seem less guilty, because King Mark trusted them so completely and because Bronwen arranged their meetings so skilfully that no one suspected them.

In public the lovers treated each other with familiar affection but no one minded that, because they had previously been friends in Ireland and were now related by marriage. The secret messages which they wove into their chit-chat gave them private pleasure without harming anyone else and the fame of King Mark's court was much enhanced by their sparkling conversation. They often played the fiddle and the harp, and composed and sang sweet songs of love. But it was thought quite proper that Tristan should sing love-songs on his lord's behalf and, when Isolt sang her lord's praises, no one doubted that she was celebrating her dutiful love for her husband, King Mark.

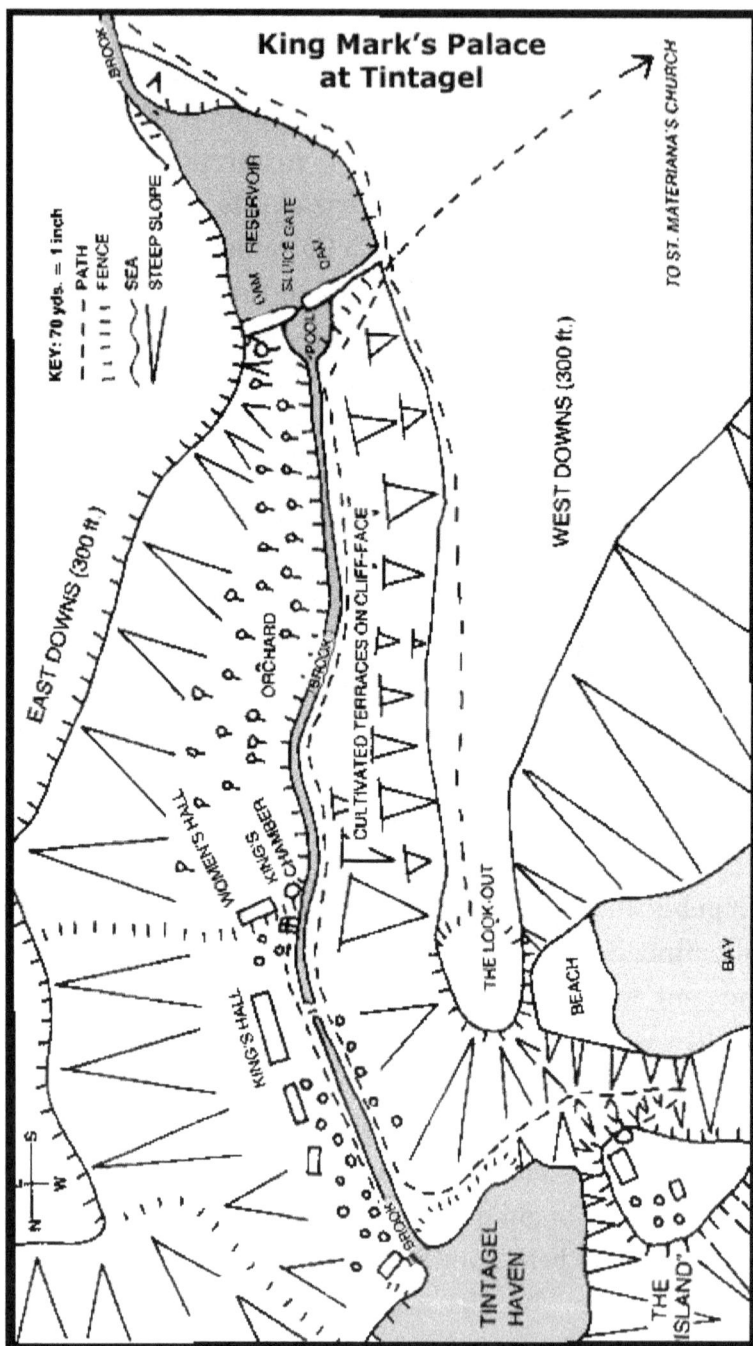

King Mark's Palace
at Tintagel

KEY: 70 yds. = 1 inch

- - - - PATH
- - - FENCE
~~~~ SEA
\\\\\\\ STEEP SLOPE

TO ST. MATERIANA'S CHURCH

BROOK

DAM RESERVOIR

SLUICE GATE

DAM

POOL

EAST DOWNS (300 ft.)

WEST DOWNS (300 ft.)

ORCHARD

BROOK

CULTIVATED TERRACES ON CLIFF-FACE

WOMEN'S HALL

KING'S
CHAMBER

KING'S HALL

THE LOOK-OUT

BEACH

BAY

BROOK

TINTAGEL
HAVEN

THE
"ISLAND"

N S E W

CHAPTER 13

THE SHADOW OF SUSPICION

A room to oneself was unheard of in Europe of 800 A.D. and no one slept by himself in the palace of Tintagel. Sometimes Tristan slept in the King's sleeping-hut, but when some other squire attended the King, Tristan shared a hut with one of his warrior-band, a young Cornish nobleman called Maddock. Maddock was an official of the King's household but he had done homage to Tristan for his arms and Tristan was more friendly with him than with any other of his sworn companions.

One winter's night, when there was no sound except the wind wailing about the crags and cliffs, Tristan and Maddock were talking in their hut. They lay in their beds, side by side, talking fitfully, until Maddock fell asleep. Then quietly and quickly Tristan got up, pulled his tunic on over his head, tied his boots around his ankles, wrapped himself in a large, dark plaid and went out.

It was a frosty night and it was very bright because of a full moon high in the sky and a light carpet of snow on the ground. But in his haste Tristan hardly noticed the beauty of the night and he needed no light, for he could have walked blindfold along the path which he took. The path wound up the valley, beside the tumbling stream, until it reached the reservoir, where the brook had been dammed to provide a reserve of water for the palace. The brook was on Tristan's left hand, as he walked towards the reservoir. Beyond the brook stood a strong, high fence, which guarded the fruit of the royal orchard from thieving hands. Below the reservoir the fence turned right and straddled the brook, in order to enclose the King's water supply from men or beasts who might foul it.

At the place where the fence crossed the stream below the outflow from the reservoir, Tristan stepped into the icy water. He twisted one of the fence palings and lifted it out. He squeezed through the gap, replaced the stake and entered the orchard. Then he made his way through the trees back towards the palace, which he had just left.

The only buildings bordering on the orchard were the King's bed-chamber and the women's quarters. All the women of the King's household slept in a single long hall but the Queen and Bronwen slept at one end of it, separated by a curtain from the other women and their children. The Queen's room had a separate door, by which she could go out to the King's hut nearby if he summoned her. Tristan hurried to this door and he scraped the wood with his fingernails in such a way that Bronwen would know who it was, although the other women would suppose that it was the gnawing of a mouse.

Maddock meanwhile had a nightmare. He dreamt that a huge black boar came from the forest and invaded the palace. Whenever anyone stood in his path, the boar pawed the ground and sharpened his tusks on his curved grinders and no one dared to await his charge. Eventually the boar in his ravaging progress reached the King's chamber. He routed the chamberlains and rushed at the rich bed, as though it was his mortal enemy. He tossed and slashed the fur-lined covers and tasselled bolsters, and he fouled the sheets with slobber and mud. Finally, when the boar had wrecked the royal bed, he ran from the palace, without anyone trying to prevent his escape.

Maddock woke up and shook his head but he was still gripped by the unpleasantness of the dream. Even when fully awake, he felt touched by doom. He wondered fearfully what the dream meant and he wanted a comforting explanation.

He whispered, "Tristan!" He called several times. He rolled over in bed and reached out to shake his friend's shoulder.

Tristan's bed was empty and Maddock found that it was quite cold inside the fur covers. Maddock suspected that Tristan had gone out on some love affair and he was resentful that his friend had not confided in him, but the longer that he thought about it, the more excited he became. Tristan's companions and the other courtiers had often joked about Tristan's lack of interest in women, for, apart from Tristan's friendly familiarity with the Queen and her ladies, no one had heard of his having anything to do at any time with any woman. Maddock was excited, because he thought that he might have found a clue to the mystery.

Maddock looked outside, to make sure that Tristan was not relieving himself or vomiting in the the lee of the hut and at once, on the moon-bright snow, he saw Tristan's tell-tale footprints. The footmarks led straight away from the hut in a purposeful manner. Maddock grinned and quickly got dressed. Although he felt ashamed of spying on his friend, he resolved to track Tristan down.

Between the black ditch of the tumbling torrent on his left and the broken hillside of cultivated terraces on his right, Maddock followed Tristan's footprints up the smooth white path. That path led out of the valley to herdsmen's huts on the downs and to other villages further away, and Maddock thought that Tristan had gone a long way for his wenching on a cold winter's night. In his haste he walked past the place where Tristan's footprints turned off the white path into the dark water, but in a while he noticed that the snow on the path in front of him was unmarked. So he turned back and soon found the loose fence-stake in the stream. Then he entered the royal orchard, following Tristan's tracks.

In the orchard Maddock went more slowly, for among the trees there was less snow and Tristan's tracks were less clear. But, when he realised where the tracks led, his heart clenched tight and he found breathing more and more difficult, as he approached the forbidden area of the private apartments of the King and Queen, for, if he was found there, his punishment would be either castration or death. Tristan's tracks, Maddock felt certain, must lead to Lady Bronwen but he himself was dragged into mortal danger by the rising tide of his own desire. Maddock had long admired the beautiful young queen and he had never before been so close to her bed.

When Maddock stopped at the edge of the orchard, he saw Tristan's tracks continuing in front of him across an open yard. The footsteps in the snow went to the women's hall, to a door which was near the King's sleeping-hut and Maddock was sure that that door would lead to the soft, warm beds of the Queen and her chief lady-in-waiting. He felt sick with longing, as he thought of Isolt's silky golden hair and smooth white skin. He could almost feel the warm, rounded softness of her body and the passionate embrace of her long, slender limbs. He gulped and stumbled forward to the door.

Maddock stood outside the door for a long while. He was listening with all his ears but he could hear nothing except the wind swishing and crackling among the bare branches of the orchard. He wondered whether to go on or to go back and he made a bargain. He told himself that, if the door was barred, he would return to his hut and would question Tristan when he came back, but he resolved that, if the door was unbarred, he would accept the opportunity and would go in to woo the Fair Isolt.

Maddock lifted the latch and pushed the door. Bronwen had forgotten to bar it. Maddock silently squeezed through the gap and quickly shut the door, feverishly hoping that neither the moonlight nor the cold air had aroused anyone. For a while he stood leaning against the door. His skin prickled and he trembled uncontrollably. But he heard no alarm and the warm smell of women gripped his throat. Little by little, his fear was banished by his desire for the lovely Isolt.

After the brightness of the moonlit snow, Maddock could at first see nothing at all in the hut but he soon made out the dark humps of two beds. He knew that the greater lady would have the bed further from the door and he crept past the bed occupied, he supposed, by Bronwen and Tristan making love. There was a faint radiance around the further bed and, in the dim light of a candle half-covered by a basket, he saw Isolt's long hair spread across the pillow. He pressed his hands against his breast to still the loud beating of his galloping heart and he tiptoed forward, yearning to pluck that lovely flower.

Then Maddock saw something else upon the pillow beside Isolt's golden hair, and even in that dim light he recognised the shape of Tristan's head. The shock was so great that he was hard put to prevent himself from crying out in anguish, but he dropped on one knee in the shadows behind the muffled candle and in a storm of jealousy he listened to the lovers' whispers. Then he crept away from the women's hall and went back to his bed.

When Tristan returned to his hut, he did not notice Maddock's footprints on the path beside his own and he slipped into bed, as he had often done before, with no suspicion that anything was amiss. The next morning he noticed without alarm that Maddock was unusually silent but, when Maddock was still surly and grim at the end of the day, Tristan began to suspect that his secret had been discovered. He warned Isolt to take great care and he himself guarded his tongue and concealed his movements.

Maddock was very jealous because Tristan had enjoyed Isolt's love, while he himself had admired and desired her only from a distance and he wanted revenge. He knew Tristan's secret but he did not dare to accuse him openly, for against an open accusation Tristan had the right to defend himself in single combat, and, like all the other Cornish nobles, Maddock was afraid of Tristan's might. Therefore Maddock worked stealthily. He told King Mark that he had heard an unpleasant rumour that Tristan was betraying his Lord with his Lord's wife and he advised the King to send Tristan away before the scandal damaged the King's honour.

King Mark dismissed the rumour with a harsh laugh. He said that he had long ago discovered that a successful man is always envied by men who are less successful; he reminded Maddock that Cornwall owed Tristan a very great debt, which was poorly repaid by evil chatter, and he commanded Maddock to try to stop the gossip. Nevertheless, King Mark could not forget the story and whenever he saw Tristan and Isolt together, he wondered whether there was any truth in it.

Against his better nature and almost against his will, King Mark tested Isolt. He tried to catch her out by cunning conversation and he summoned her to him suddenly and at all times of the day and night. Isolt avoided all the King's snares and she served him loyally and lovingly. But the unlucky King found that the ghost of his suspected rival always lay between him and his wife, and though he desired her ever more urgently, he could no longer enjoy her company.

One night, as the King and Queen lay in the big royal bed, King Mark sighed and said, "Lady, I have been advised to go as a pilgrim to Rome, in order to purge my soul of a grief which lies heavy upon it. While I am away, who should be in charge of the kingdom and of my household?"

Without thinking, Isolt answered, "I should not have thought that that would be much of a problem, My Lord. Apart from you there is only one man whom all Cornishmen obey. That is the Lord Tristan, your heir presumptive."

This answer increased King Mark's suspicions and he thought, *She wants to get rid of me and to be left in Tristan's charge.*

He was quite right. In the morning Isolt skipped back to her room and told Bronwen excitedly, "The King is going away for a long time and I think that he will leave both me and the kingdom in Tristan's charge."

But wiser Bronwen whispered anxiously, "Tell me precisely everything that was said both by the King and by yourself. I fear that you may have walked into a trap." And, when she had heard about the King's question, she advised Isolt how to answer if the King ever again mentioned his pilgrimage.

Another night, the King embraced Isolt and whispered in her ear, "Lovely one, nothing on this earth is dearer to me than you. How shall I be able to live without you when I go on my pilgrimage?"

Then Isolt began to weep. "I thought that your talk of going on a pilgrimage was only a joke," she said. "If you really mean to leave me so soon, you cannot love me much. It is less than a year since you stole me from my parents' home and taught me to love you and already you talk of leaving me unloved and alone in a strange land."

"But lovely one!" King Mark cried. "You yourself asked to be left in Tristan's charge. You know him well and, as you said, no Cornishman will dare to hurt you while he is here."

"Oh, Sire!" wailed Isolt, "I only said that because I thought that you would like to leave Tristan in charge. I hate him. He killed my uncle and, in spite of the alliance and all the peace-making, my uncle's death has not yet been avenged. Tristan knows how I feel. As soon as you are out of the way, he will abandon his pretence of politeness and he will slaughter me, as he did my uncle. Take me with you, my beloved master. I will go anywhere with you."

For a few days King Mark was happy and contented, but the doubts returned and yet again he tested his wife. In the silent darkness of the night and in the privacy of their bed he told her, "Dear love, I have decided that we cannot both of us leave the kingdom at the same time and for so long. Therefore, since I must go, you must stay here. I myself believe that Tristan is too loyal to ill-treat my wife, but to avoid the problem which you fear, I shall send him away. He can go back to Lothian."

"Thank you, My Dear Lord!" Isolt cried. But after a pause she said, "If you can do a lot for me, I can do a little for you. If for my sake you can banish your nephew, for your sake I can put up with him. Now that I am assured that you love me enough to take my part against Lord Tristan, I can defend myself against his ill-will. I know as well as you do that there is no one so suited to be your regent as Tristan, for he has served you well and he is loved by all the common people. If Tristan is in charge while you are away, you will feel confident that your enemies will neither seize your lands nor rebel against you, but if you banish him, the people will blame me because of the blood-feud following Morolt's death"

Isolt praised Tristan no more than was his due but, because she spoke in Tristan's favour, the King distrusted her and doubt grew in his heart. Isolt soon noticed it and the next night, when she went to his bed, she put her arms around his neck and whispered softly, "My Dear Lord, have you yet arranged for Tristan to go back to his homeland? If you do that before you leave me to go on your pilgrimage, I shall be most grateful. I was too rash yesterday when I offered to bear with Tristan for your sake. My heart fails me. I should be frightened to be under his rule without you here to protect me.

"If you do not want to banish Tristan because I should be blamed, take him with you on your pilgrimage. Perhaps Maddock could keep Cornwall safe, while you and Tristan are away. The best of all would be if you left Tristan here and took me with you. That is what I myself would like best. But all the same, I shall submit to your will in this, as in everything. I only want to please you, My Own Dear Lord."

CHAPTER 14

THE SHADOWS LENGTHEN

For two months King Mark almost forgot his suspicions about Tristan and Isolt. Isolt served him as a loving wife should and to Tristan she was distantly polite. The lovers avoided crossing glances and in company they rarely spoke together. It was painful for them to pretend to be enemies in public but for that price they could enjoy their love in private and they often met under cover of the dark in the Queen's quarters.

Maddock was quite out of favour with both Tristan and King Mark and he had no opportunity to spy on Tristan. But he believed that the lovers continued to meet and he tried to revive the King's suspicions. He bribed the King's dwarfish jester, a Breton called Mellot, to spy on the lovers and to taunt the King and this Mellot could do, because he often entered both the King's chamber and the women's hall in order to amuse his lord and lady.

Tristan and Isolt were less guarded in their looks and words when they were together in the women's hall and Mellot soon saw that they behaved like lovers, sitting silent with entangled eyes, brushing hands and singing love-songs with passionate tenderness. When the little jester was sure of his suspicions, he began to taunt the King. He told funny stories about old men with flighty young wives and he made jokes about "trusting Tristan as far as you can see Isolt" and about Tristan's badge, the boar. One little rhyme which Mellot often sang went like this: "She saw the boar; 'E sought the sow. The boar she saw has topped her now."

When Mellot saw that his jesting had aroused the King's jealousy, he dared to advise him in another rhyme: "Unless you chase The boar you fed, He'll take your place at board and bed."

The King was tormented by his suspicions and he decided that it would be better to know the worst than to continue in such an agony of doubt. He resolved to test his suspicions and Mellot's rhymes gave him the idea for a cunning trap. King Mark told Tristan that he had news that the King of Wessex on his eastern borders intended to attack Cornwall and he commanded him to enlarge the fortress on the Island, so that, if necessary, the whole royal household could take refuge there. Tristan gathered a gang of slaves and peasants and set them to build a tall, round stone tower and a new timber hall on the Island. He had intended to sleep in the palace and to cross the causeway to the Island every day to supervise the work but the King told him that, only if he actually lived on the Island, could he really find out what supplies would be needed to withstand a siege and finally the King commanded him to live on the Island and never to return to the mainland until the job was finished.

Tristan worked furiously, to finish his task as quickly as possible, for his longing for Isolt constantly increased, as the sun's heat increased with the summer. But, whenever the King came to see the progress of the work, he suggested further alterations or additions and Tristan was barred from Isolt's arms for three whole months. Tristan grew lean and heavy-eyed and Isolt grew pale and gaunt. They were starved of love.

When King Mark saw Tristan and Isolt pining, he thought that his plan was succeeding. Then early in July, when the male deer are well-fleshed before the breeding season, King Mark gave out that he would be away from Tintagel for three weeks' hunting.

Tristan ought to have accompanied the King but, as King Mark had expected, Tristan pleaded sickness. Angrily the King commanded Tristan to stay on the Island and he told Mellot, the dwarf, to note and report all Tristan's movements. The King was sure that, if Tristan and Isolt truly were lovers, they would try to meet while he was away and he wanted to catch them in the act.

Bronwen came to the Island, to talk to Tristan on Isold's behalf. The lovers suspected that Mellot and others were spying on them but they felt that, unless they met soon, they would die. So a signal was agreed. When the women saw freshly cut chips of wood floating down the stream past their quarters, Tristan would be waiting by the reservoir. The lover's trysting-place, it was agreed, would be the big, old apple tree hanging over the pool below the reservoir, for that tree provided a dark and sheltered place within the orchard fence and the rushing waterfall would cover their voices.

The causeway joining the Island to the mainland was guarded and Mellot kept watch in the look-out above it. But lovelorn Tristan was both strong and desperate. In the moonlight he climbed down the precipitous side of the Island, swam the swirling sea and climbed up the high cliffs of the mainland to Saint Materiana's Church. Then he made his way unseen to the head of the valley, crept past the reservoir, removed the loose paling and broke into the royal orchard.

Tristan squatted beneath the apple tree, cutting chips of wood into the flowing stream. There Isolt found him and then at last the starving lovers obtained the nourishment which they needed.

Mellot, King Mark's spy, was baffled for five days. Every night Tristan left his bed on the Island but every morning he was found sleeping in his proper place. On the sixth night Mellot decided to try to catch Tristan by keeping an eye on Isolt. He hid himself in the King's sleeping-hut, to watch the women's hall. As soon as the moon rose and lightened the night, two figures left the women's hall and stood near the stream. They were heavily wrapped in cowled cloaks against both the cold air and prying eyes but Mellot thought that they were of the height and slimness of Isolt and Bronwen.

The two women stood as still as statues for a long while and Mellot began to get sleepy. But suddenly one woman pointed into the stream and the other hurried away through the apple trees up towards the reservoir. Mellot could not follow the woman who had vanished into the shadowy orchard, because the other woman kept guard between the palace and the orchard but he resolved that the next night he would keep watch at the top of the orchard, in the hope of finding the lovers' trysting place.

On the seventh evening after King Mark's departure, Mellot hid himself beside the earth wall which dammed the reservoir. He saw the shadowy figure of a tall man appear from nowhere and squat beside the pool and a little later he saw the man get up and hurry to meet a woman who came through the trees. The spying dwarf could not see for certain who the man and woman were but they flew into each other's arms and lay close together in the black shadows of the apple tree beside the pool. When the moon was going down the sky, the man escorted the woman back through the orchard, returned alone to the pool and disappeared suddenly through the fence.

The next morning Mellot reported his discovery to King Mark and the King told him to try to trap Tristan by pretending to be a messenger from Isolt. So Mellot went to Tristan, where he was directing the building on the Island, and whispered behind his hand, "Lord Tristan, please listen. I have a message for you. The lovely woman asks you to meet her tonight at the same place as last night. The Fair One requires you not to fail her tonight."

"I am in no mood for your jests," Tristan said crossly. "Go away!"

"Yes indeed, Sir!" answered the dwarf. "Many people in the

court blame me for helping your game with the Queen and I should be punished, if it was known that I had carried a message between you."

"I don't know what you are talking about but, if there is evil gossip in the court, I expect it was you who invented it. Therefore go away"

"Lord Tristan, give me your answer, for I must hurry back to the lovely woman."

"If my honour would permit me to strike such an ugly little runt, you would have an answer which would never reach the mainland," Tristan said fiercely. "Now leave me, before I lose my patience."

Mellot's trap had failed but he persuaded the King to return to Tintagel after dark and to keep watch in the apple tree beneath which the lovers had met the previous night. The King and his dwarf sat in the branches for some hours and the elderly King was already cramped and ill-tempered, when suddenly he saw a shadow dark on the moonlit fence. The shadow moved and it crouched small over the stream. The dwarf showed the King by gestures that Tristan was cutting chips of wood into the water and that the Queen would come to meet him. Still without a sound, the shadow straightened up and stood beside the pool. Tristan looked down at the moonlit water, dappled with the shadow of the big old apple tree hanging over it. The leaves and twigs waved lightly in the wind and their shadows shifted. But two more massive shadows did not move in the wind and, without looking up, Tristan knew that there were two men in the tree above him. With a lurch of his belly, he understood instantly that Isolt and he were in mortal danger.

"God save Isolt!" Tristan cried but, although his heart shouted that prayer to Heaven, his lips did not repeat his heart's agonised cry. He uttered no sound but he turned with stiff, leaden limbs, to watch Isolt coming through the trees. She would soon be dead, unless he could warn her.

At the edge of the orchard Isolt halted. Never before had Tristan failed to run forward to meet her at that point but tonight he stood like a statue, like a stag frozen with awareness of danger and Isolt the eager lover became Isolt the wary prey. She looked around her; she sniffed the air; she listened with ears like trumpets but she kept her distance from Tristan.

"Gracious Queen!" Tristan called in an embarrassed voice. "There is a strange fish in this pool tonight." That made Isolt look down and outlined on the grass between Tristan and herself she saw the shadows of three men —Tristan and two others. At once she felt the trap and, without evidence but with complete certainty, she knew that the King, her husband, was watching her closely.

"It is a fish which I know well," she answered coldly and went on in icy tones: "What is it that you have to say to me, Lord Tristan? By calling me out here at this time of night you have endangered not only your own honour and mine but also that of My Dear Lord, the King. Surely you are aware of the wicked tales which that viper Mellot has been spreading. That treacherous dwarf and your false friend Maddock have been putting it about that you and I are lovers. If My Lord and husband heard that we had met at this time of night, he might believe the tale.

If My Lord accuses me, I shall swear on his most sacred relics that I never loved any man except him who had my maidenhead and I can trust My Lord to believe me, for he well knows that I have always served him as a loyal and loving wife. But the prattling of the cowardly courtiers will never be still, for you and I are both foreigners here and, even though I am at feud with you because you slew my uncle, they nonetheless couple our names together and call us lovers. Whatever happens, these Cornishmen will try to discredit us, because they envy us."

"Gracious Queen!" Tristan answered humbly. "It is for that very reason that I dared to ask you to be good enough to speak to me privately. I know well how Maddock and Mellot make the Cornish courtiers smirk and giggle by telling tales to our shame and My Good Lord's dishonour and I can see no way to save the King's honour from these snakes' tongues, unless I leave the court. I propose, therefore, to ask the King to let me depart in a week's time and truthfully, although I shall be sad at leaving My Lord and although his throne will be less secure because of my departure, I shall not be sorry to go. For I am hurt by the ungrateful spite of the Cornish chiefs, whom I have saved from shame and slavery and my life here is made intolerable by the King's suspicion and by your undying hatred, Gracious Lady, because to save Cornwall I killed your uncle.

"My request, Gracious Queen, is that you and the King will pretend to like me for the few days that I shall stay in Cornwall. Otherwise, my departure will seem to be caused by the ill will of either you or the King. The courtiers will say: 'Isolt pursues her feud and betrays her kiss of peace' or 'Perhaps after all there was some truth in Mellot's funny stories about a love affair between the King's wife and his nephew.'

"Finally," said Tristan: "the world at large will think that My Lord acted most ungratefully in banishing me. For they will remember that I alone saved his kingdom from the shameful tribute and they will remember that I alone healed the ancient war between King Angus and him with a marriage alliance."

Isolt thought for a while. Then she said, "Lord Tristan, I cannot pretend that I myself shall be sorry to see the back of Morolt's murderer. Nevertheless, honesty forces me to admit that you have been vilely treated by the King and chieftains of Cornwall, for their good reputation is entirely due to you and they have done nothing but whisper and plot against you. I therefore undertake to treat you as a well-loved kinsman until your departure. But I cannot safely speak to the King on your behalf, for, whenever I tell him anything favourable to you, he suspects that Mellot's lying tales are true. Whatever happens, Lord Tristan, may the Mother of God watch over you!"

"May Heaven bless you, Gracious Queen! And, if we never meet again, I pray God to keep you safe in both life and reputation."

So Tristan and Isolt parted, with never a kiss and never a touch of the hand. They went to their beds, with their eyes dimmed by tears and their hearts heavy with grief. They did not know how much King Mark knew about their love; nor did they know whether their play-acting had convinced him. They could only wait and see what he did next, for they were helpless in his hands.

King Mark climbed down from the apple tree. He was stiff and sore and also racked by remorse for his unjust suspicions of his dear wife and nephew but some of his misery he worked off on Mellot. He thrashed the dwarf with his whip, until the rocks rang with the dwarf's screams. Then he rode through the night back to his hunting lodge.

The King slept badly, turning over in his mind all that he had heard while hiding in the tree. He could hardly wait till daylight before riding home to test Isolt with his secret knowledge.

"How have you been, Dear Lady?" he asked her, when she came before him.

"I have spent the days with sadness, My Lord, and the nights with sorrow" Isolt answered vaguely.

"What do you mean?"

"I have been sorry without reason and sad without cause. That is all, Sire."

"Humph!" King Mark grunted and he thought of the reasons for grief which she had mentioned the previous night. "How is

Tristan?" he asked. "When I left to go hunting a week ago, he said that he was unwell."

"Yesterday he was both unwell and unhappy," Isolt answered but she added quickly, "So I heard."

"Did Tristan tell you that himself, Lady?"

"He told Bronwen, Sire. Although Bronwen was related to Morolt, she does not bear a grudge against Tristan for Morolt's death, as I do and she went to the Island to see how Tristan was. She told me that he looked very ill and she brought me a message from him."

"Oh! What was that?" the King asked.

"Tristan asked me and you also, Sire, to hide our hatred of him for just one week. He wants to leave Cornwall, without giving grounds for people to say that you and I are sending him away."

"So he wants to leave us. What else did he say?"

Isolt repeated all that Tristan had said the previous night in King Mark's hearing and the King believed in her good faith. He was sad and remorseful and he kept hammering his right fist into the palm of his left hand. At last he begged Isolt, "If you love me, Lady, bring us together again. Be the bridge between Tristan and me. I have been tempted by liars and tricksters to suspect him unjustly of disloyalty."

With a show of reluctance Isolt answered sharply, "I can see that your honour and advantage make it desirable to keep Tristan here, for he is the kingpost of this country of cowards and vile slanderers and without him Cornwall is not worth much. But he is my enemy and I should be glad to see him go."

"Lady!" King Mark said very humbly, "I understand how you feel about Tristan but he used to be my closest friend. Please help me to make my peace with him."

"What is the point in my helping you to make peace with Tristan?" Isolt asked bitterly. "For tomorrow you will be at his throat again with your dishonourable and disloyal suspicions."

"Never again, Fair Isolt! Both Tristan and you are safe forever from my suspicions," King Mark assured her. "I know now how it is between you and I will never again suspect you of betraying me because for my sake you make an outward show of family affection."

King Mark tried hard to forget his suspicions and he treated Tristan and Isolt with trusting affection, as in the early days. But doubts are like weeds. However often they are hoed out and burnt, their seeds remain and breed a new crop. So it was with King Mark. He showed complete trust in Tristan and Isolt but in his heart he wondered and behind his smiling face he prepared another trap.

One evening the King had himself and his wife bled and for company, he had Tristan and Bronwen bled all at the same time. After the surgeon had gone, they lay on three beds in the King's sleeping-hut with their arms bandaged. Then during the night, when the bell sounded for the midnight Vigils, King Mark called Mellot the dwarf to help him dress and to escort him to his chapel nearby. But Mellot had been told in advance to sprinkle flour on the floor around the King's bed before following the King to his prayers.

Watchful Bronwen saw the trick and warned Tristan not to try to join Isolt in the King's bed. But Tristan was aflame with love for the Queen and he stood up on his bed and leapt across the three yard space to the King's bed. In the exertion of that great leap the bandage on his arm was torn loose and the new scab on his bleeding-point was broken open. The passionate lovers noticed nothing amiss and Tristan jumped back to his own bed, before King Mark returned. But the King found his sheets dappled and streaked with blood and he asked Isolt sternly: "Where did all this blood come from, My Lady?"

"Sire, my vein opened, when I turned in my sleep," Isolt said and she showed him where at that very instant she had ripped her bandage.

The King could see that there were no footmarks except his own on the floor near his bed but he found Isolt's story difficult to believe and he strode across to Tristan's bed, saying as though in fun, "Get up, Tristan. It is not right that the squire should be loafing in bed, when his lord is up."

King Mark stripped back the covers and gazed down at Tristan's naked form. Both Tristan and his bedclothes were plentifully smeared with fresh blood. The King's face set in bitter lines of hatred and misery. Now he felt that he <u>knew</u> the truth but he realised that the evidence was not strong enough to convict. He felt sure that Tristan had been in bed with Isolt but he could not prove it; indeed the unmarked floor around his bed was evidence in Tristan's favour.

"Tristan, I give you leave to depart from Cornwall" King Mark said in icy tones. "In this kingdom there is not enough room for both you and me and, if you remain here, there will be no honour either for you or for me or for Isolt."

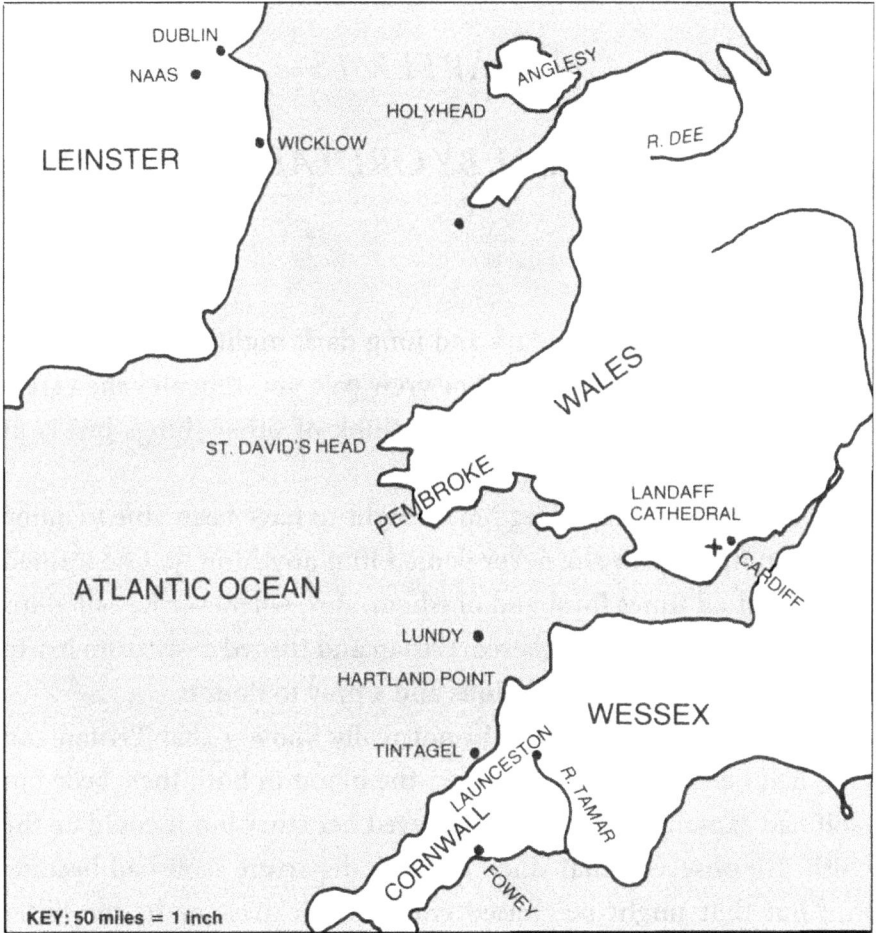

KEY: 50 miles = 1 inch

DUBLIN
NAAS
LEINSTER
WICKLOW
HOLYHEAD
ANGLESY
R. DEE
WALES
ST. DAVID'S HEAD
PEMBROKE
LANDAFF
CATHEDRAL
CARDIFF
ATLANTIC OCEAN
LUNDY
HARTLAND POINT
WESSEX
TINTAGEL
LAUNCESTON
R. TAMAR
CORNWALL
FOWEY

CHAPTER 15

TRIAL BY ORDEAL

Through the stormy days and long dark nights of winter, Isolt pined for her banished lover. She grew pale and thin and she rarely smiled. Bronwen tried to make her think of other things but Isolt thought about Tristan all the time.

With Tristan away, King Mark ought to have been able to enjoy Isolt's company, for she never denied him anything that he wanted and was at all times loyal and obedient. But, whenever he called his wife to his bed, he remembered Tristan and turned away from her in bitter anger. He was both jealous and a prey to doubts.

King Mark knew —but did not really know— that Tristan and Isolt had been lovers. He had seen the blood in both their beds but Isolt had explained that. He disbelieved her story but it could be the truth. He observed that since Tristan's departure Isolt had become thin but that might be caused either by sickness or by the bitter weather. He remembered that only twelve months ago he had loved Tristan and Isolt more than anyone else in the world. Sometimes he loved them still, but more often he hated them.

King Mark's doubts were fed by the spate of stories going round his court. During the winter, when everybody was indoors a good part of the time, the conversation in a chief's crowded hall always took a sharper edge and a more slanderous turn and in King Mark's palace, when Tristan was not there to protect his good name, tales multiplied about his love affair with Isolt. Most of the tales were based on guesswork, because no one except faithful Bronwen knew anything for certain. Nevertheless, the honour of the King and Queen was sadly damaged and King Mark was forced to take action.

When the Cornish chiefs gathered at Tintagel for the Christmas court, King Mark asked them how he ought to deal with the harmful rumours. They advised him to deny the rumours firmly and to punish anyone who repeated them, but he replied that he could not deny what he suspected was true. They advised him to try Tristan and Isolt in open court but he said that in spite of his enquiries, he had never found evidence enough to convict them. They advised him to find a champion who would publicly declare that Tristan was a traitor to his lord, but he asked who would dare to accuse Tristan, since Tristan would have the right of trial by combat.

Many made speeches but no one offered a workable solution of the King's problem, until an old abbot spoke. "Sire, to stop the rumours which are damaging the reputations of yourself and the Queen, you must first discover the truth of the matter. Once you know the truth, you can punish everyone who repeats false tales. From what you have told us, it seems that only Lord Tristan and Queen Isolt themselves know the truth. So, for your honour's sake, they, or one of them, must be compelled to declare the truth of their relationship.

"Lord King, it is clear that neither you nor anyone in Cornwall can discover the truth through the Lord Tristan. In the first place he is not here to tell us; in the second place this kingdom owes him such a debt of gratitude that it would be shameful to accuse him without positive proof; in the third place, if he were accused, he would have the right to defend himself in battle, and we know of no one who would dare fight him.

"Therefore, My Lord, you must come at the truth through the Fair Isolt, your Gracious Queen. I advise you to call her before you in your council. Then, if you give me leave and if God helps me, I undertake to bring the matter to a conclusion one way or the other."

The King summoned his wife and, when she stood before him in his council, he commanded her to take a seat and to answer truthfully the abbot's questions. The abbot bowed to Isolt and said, "Lady Isolt, Gracious Queen, please bear me no ill will for what I am about to say. Lady, the King has told us —and indeed we all know it— that his honour is menaced by a strong and widespread rumour. That rumour links you with the King's nephew. To protect the honour both of the King and of yourself, and to protect the honour of the Lord Tristan also, the truth must be known. I therefore advise you to declare in the hearing of the King and his council whether there is any truth in the allegations"

Isolt proudly answered the abbot by addressing the King. "Sire, before your council I declare that it is not a queen's duty to meddle in the gossip of her lord's court and no woman should be expected to defend herself against the unsupported slander of dwarfs and false friends. But, Lord King, you can be sure that I shall always be ready to defend your honour, and my own, against direct accusations of disloyalty."

"Lady Queen!" the abbot said sternly, "The allegations are so widespread that I must myself make a formal accusation that you have acted treasonably to your Lord, the King, and I solemnly require you, for the sake of the King's good name, to declare whether or not you are innocent. Until you are cleared of this accusation, I advise the King to bar you from his bed and board."

"My Dear Lord!" Isolt cried, falling on her knees at the King's feet. "I will prove my innocence on any sacred relics that you choose and by any ordeal that satisfies you."

Then the good abbot advised the King, "Sire, since there is no evidence to substantiate the charge, you can ask of your Queen nothing more than the satisfaction which she has offered and I advise you, Sire, to fix a day and a place for the trial by ordeal. Anyone who repeats slanderous rumours about the Queen in the meantime should be imprisoned. They can be judged later, according to the outcome of the Queen's trial."

"I agree," the King said. "Lady, I require a pledge that you will appear in Llandaff Cathedral near Cardiff at Candlemas, the second of February, for trial by the ordeal of red-hot iron." Isolt handed the King a gold ring and promised to appear for trial. She held her head high, as she walked with slow and stately steps from the King's hall but, once she reached her room and found the comfort of Bronwen's bosom, she broke down and sobbed in helpless fear.

You, who read this story, don't be too hard on Isolt. She was only fifteen years old and far from her family and fellow countrymen, far also from her lover Tristan, and in her desperation she had chosen to delay death for a while by rashly offering to prove her innocence in the sight of God, who knows all things. No mention had been made of the penalty if she failed in the trial but a queen who betrayed her lord must expect some spectacular and shameful death, like being burned alive, or being torn to pieces by wild horses. Isolt herself knew just how far she was from the innocence which she must swear on sacred relics and prove by carrying the blessed, burning iron.

During the five weeks between Christmas and Candlemas Isolt threw herself on God's mercy. She prayed often and confessed to her chaplain every trifling sin except her unlawful love. Often she thought that she felt the red-hot iron searing her hands; often in imagination she lay bound on a hurdle over a brushwood fire and felt the flames licking at her ribs, and often in her dreams she felt the wrenching of her arms and legs, as plunging horses dragged her body apart. She knew that she was guilty in the sight of God, even if the truth was hidden from men, but she was an ever-faithful lover and not once did she offer to give up Tristan in return for God's help at the terrifying trial.

Isolt never promised God not to do it again, for she fully intended to do it again, just as soon and as often as circumstances allowed. But she prayed both for courage and for cunning; she gave alms to the poor and gifts to the church, and one day, while on her knees in the King's chapel, she had an inspiration. She jumped up from the altar-step and ran to write a letter to Tristan. She told him to come without fail to Cardiff at Candlemas and she told him what he must do there, if he wished to save her.

On Candlemas morning the ship carrying the King and Great Men of Cornwall and the one carrying Isolt and her attendant women sailed into Cardiff to land their passengers. When King Mark and the Cornish chiefs had waded ashore, the Queen's ship was poled as close to the beach as it could get and a Cornish squire stepped into the sea, to carry his queen to land. But Isolt saw an Irish pilgrim among the crowd and she called out, "On this day, when I shall soon stand before the Heavenly Throne to prove my innocence, I should rather be carried by a holy man from my own country. Ask that Irish pilgrim to be my porter. Ask that old beggar, if he has the strength, to bear me to the shore."

In the crowd of sightseers the Cornish courtiers saw a dirty old man wearing a yellow and brown chequered Irish plaid and they saw that a pilgrim's palm fronds were fastened to his hood. They did not recognise Tristan beneath the dirt and humble clothes and they shouted, "Come here, old man and carry the Queen ashore. It is not often that a beggar can cuddle a queen; so step forward and grasp your good luck."

Tristan put down his staff and waded into the sea. He took Isolt in his arms and carried her slowly to the shore. He felt her trembling with fear of the ordeal but she felt him trembling with violent love-longing. Then Isolt laughed triumphantly, for his love had driven out her fear. In Tristan's loving arms she could do anything. ANYTHING! She could trick them all and perhaps, if God would allow it, she could trick even Him.

"Fall on the ground with me, as soon as we reach land," Isolt whispered and obediently Tristan stumbled and fell down with Isolt still clasped closely in his arms. The courtiers ran forward to drag the dirty pilgrim off their queen.

"Beat him. Beat him for dishonouring the Queen," the courtiers cried and they began to do so. But Isolt shouted out, "No, no! Stop it. He has dishonoured me less than you courtiers, for he has soiled only my clothes; whereas you have soiled my name and reputation. The pilgrim bore me no malice and I forgive him his unintentional mistake. It is those who have deliberately slandered me with filthy lies who deserve to be punished." Isolt stared keenly at her husband, until King Mark lowered his eyes in shame.

Isolt told her chamberlain to give the pilgrim a reward from her chest. What she gave Tristan was a wooden begging-bowl and that bowl was the one from which eighteen months previously they had drunk the love potion together.

On the way to the cathedral Isolt reminded the King about the comic incident of the Irish pilgrim, for several times she said, "Now I shall be hard put to swear on oath that none but my husband has held me in his arms. Ayah! That dirty pilgrim has held me in his arms as close as has the King."

When they reached the cathedral at Llandaff, Bronwen prepared Isolt for the holy trial. She lifted off Isolt's golden circlet and unbraided the gold threads from her hair. She took off Isolt's embroidered purple cloak and stripped off her fine cloth tunic and silken gown, her stockings and leather shoes. Isolt gave all her finery and jewels to the poor who were begging alms outside the cathedral.

She herself stood barefoot in a rough woollen smock which reached only to her knees; her golden hair hung unconfined over her shoulders and down to her waist and, as she walked, she held before her the candle of a penitent.

As Isolt walked up the cathedral to hear Mass at the sanctuary step, many of those who watched, wept to see such beauty humbled and in fear of death and King Mark felt his heart squeezed small between his hatred and his love for her. But Maddock and Mellot licked their lips like gluttons, for they were greedy for the vengeance which would soon be theirs and they rejoiced to see the heavy bar of iron already growing hot over a brazier of glowing coals.

When Isolt had heard Mass and had prayed boldly to be saved from shame, she was led to the table where the holy relics lay in golden caskets. Without hesitation she stretched her hands over the relics and spoke to the King. "Now, Sire!" she said, "Tell me what form of oath you wish me to swear."

But the King had not made up his mind and it seemed as though all the important people in the cathedral were offering their advice. At last Isolt herself shouted above the din of conflicting opinion, "Sire, listen to the oath which I shall swear and, if it does not satisfy you, tell me how to better it, for it is <u>tou</u> who needs to be assured of my innocence and it is <u>your</u> doubts alone which have brought me to this shameful pass.

"In the presence of Almighty God and before this assembly I swear upon these holy relics that no man ever lay with me and held me in his arms except you, my lord, and that poor beggar who carried me ashore this morning. So help me God and all His saints to an honourable end to my ordeal!"

King Mark sat thinking for a while and all the people were utterly silent, for after the oath must come the cruel ordeal. At last the King said, "Yes! If you can carry the red-hot iron to the altar upon that oath, I shall be satisfied and may God show forth the truth!"

Isolt walked forward to the glowing brazier of red-hot coals, which in that dark church sparked and shimmered like a living light. Her face was whiter than her smock; her steps were unsteady and her breast rose and fell rapidly with every panting breath. There was a long groan from the crowd and many people promised a candle to their patron saint, asking for heavenly help for the unlucky lady in her desperate need. Even King Mark felt pity for her youth and beauty, when she stood alone before the red-hot iron.

Tristan clenched his teeth, until his jaw muscles stood out like knots in his cheeks; he gripped his shoulders beneath his plaid, until his nails drew blood; his skin crawled and his hair bristled with abject horror of the burning iron. But Isolt calmly tucked her hair behind her ears and rolled her sleeves above her elbows. Both Tristan and Isolt closed their eyes briefly, to say a final prayer. But he thought only of Isolt and how they had shared the fatal loving-cup and she thought only of Tristan and how he had trembled with urgent longing when he carried her from her ship.

"Hah!" said Isolt exultantly, and held out her hands, palm upwards, towards the bishop who stood at the brazier. The bishop blessed the iron bar and called on God to burn the Queen if her oath was false. Then with a pair of tongs he gripped the glowing bar and held it high.

The brightness of the bar kindled the staring eyes of the crowd in the church like stars in a dark sky and painted Isolt's face with ruddy gold. The musty church stank with the rancid reek of Man's ancient terror for agonising, all-destroying fire, as the gentle bishop laid the red-hot iron on Isolt's outstretched hands.

A loud sigh went up from the crowd, for many accused persons dropped the iron at once, when it scorched their hands unbearably. But Isolt had stood firm, as though she felt no pain and then she turned and walked steadily towards the altar. Isolt was shivering, not with fear but with immortality, for she felt as though she was no longer flesh and blood but only spirit— pure, loving spirit. She felt at peace with the world and she hated no one, not even Maddock or Mellot. Her heart was full of love and at the very heart of her boundless love was Tristan.

Isolt reached the altar and lowered the iron into the basin of holy water which had been put there to receive it. The water spat and sizzled and steam rose to the roof. But Isolt held up her hands, white and unmarked.

The bishop examined Isolt's hands and praised God for revealing the truth so wonderfully. The King wept over her hands and wiped his tears away with kisses. The little miracle had turned him upside down. It had swept away all his suspicions and all his doubts. It had brought him back to the unquestioning love of his early married life.

The King himself led Isolt to the seat beside his own and he called for her robes of state and for her crown. But she firmly refused to wear her crown, until the King had sworn on the holy relics that he truly believed that she was innocent and very humbly King Mark did so.

While the Great Men and the courtiers were congratulating Isolt and while the people were cheering to the sky, she looked only for her lover's face among the crowd. It was not hard to find, for in all that cheering, laughing, waving mob only Tristan was still and his face was haggard with the horror and wonder of what he had just seen.

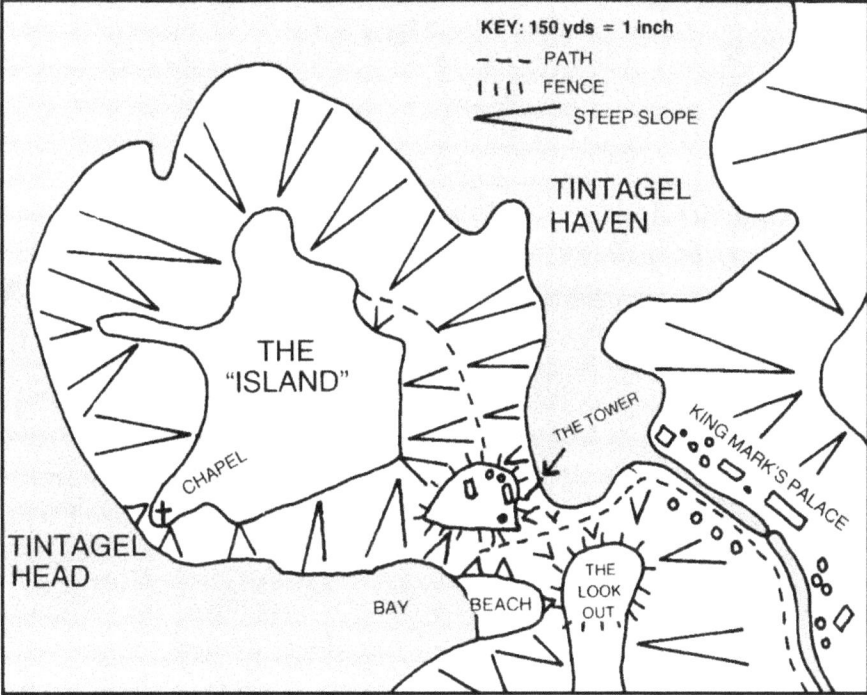

KEY: 150 yds = 1 inch
- - - PATH
ꞮꞮꞮꞮ FENCE
STEEP SLOPE

TINTAGEL
HAVEN

THE
"ISLAND"

THE TOWER

KING MARK'S PALACE

CHAPEL

TINTAGEL
HEAD

THE
LOOK
OUT

BAY

BEACH

CHAPTER 16

TRISTAN'S LEAP

King Mark truly believed in Isolt's innocence, because he had seen it "proved" before God by the terrible ordeal, and as he settled back into his comfortable life with Isolt in his bed and at his board, he soon wanted the company of his other friend, Tristan. In his heart King Mark loved and admired Tristan, and if Isolt was innocent, then Tristan must be innocent. So he sent messengers to find Tristan to invite him back to Tintagel and when Tristan's ship arrived in the haven, the King himself went down and welcomed him warmly with a kinsman's kisses.

Whatever King Mark did, he was never long out of the company of his two dearest friends. In all his life, since his sister eloped with Tristan's father, he had never loved anyone except those two, but he could clearly see that the ties which bound Tristan and Isolt together were stronger than those which bound either of them to himself. Often he observed a tender, loving glance, which flashed between them when they thought that he was not looking. Often he noticed that their hands lay together on a seat or dipped at the same time into a bowl of food. Often he wondered, when neither was in sight, whether they were together.

King Mark managed to subdue his jealousy and he taught himself to accept the fact that Tristan and Isolt loved each other at least as much as they each loved him. Indeed he realised that the three of them were bound more firmly, because each of them loved the other two, than they would have been if Tristan and Isolt were competing for his love. But, however he reasoned, he could not bear to think of Tristan and Isolt lying together in naked love.

Because King Mark had now accepted that Tristan and Isolt were in love, he did not dare to risk an open quarrel by forbidding them to be alone together; nor did he want to catch them out in an act of unlawful love. He wanted above all to banish from his mind the thought of them lying in bed together and he did his best to prevent it happening. The fence enclosing the King's chamber, the women's quarters and the orchard, was strengthened and inspected daily, and the only gate into that private compound was guarded night and day by armed sentries.

Tristan and Isolt were starved of love and they pined away. Their cheeks became pale, their movements listless and their eyes revealed the misery of their hearts. King Mark saw their plight and he felt both distress at his friends' sadness and jealousy at its cause. But he told himself that he had tamed his jealousy for their sakes so they should learn to forego love-making for his sake. Nevertheless, whatever King Mark thought, neither the lovers' desire nor his own jealousy could be controlled by sheer will power, and their will power soon became the servant of their emotions.

Tristan needed Isolt with such burning urgency that he resolved to climb down a precipice into the royal orchard. But he would be exposed on the rock face a few yards from a sentry, and he could therefore make the dangerous journey only on stormy nights when the moon would be obscured by cloud, and the howling wind would drown the clatter of falling stones. It was desperately risky but the desperate lovers would take any risk for the sake of a meeting. Secretly and from afar, Tristan studied the cliff in the bright light of day. He tried to memorise each foothold and each handhold which he must find in the pitch dark and against the buffeting of stormy wind and rain.

One day King Mark noticed that Tristan and Isolt seemed suddenly less sad. He soon guessed the reason and his bitter jealousy compelled him to order Maddock and twenty armed men to hide in the orchard, in case "someone" might find a way to the women's quarters. When next Tristan climbed down to the women's hall, Maddock's men set upon him at the Queen's door. Tristan was wearing no defensive armour but he was determined not to endanger her by being captured near her and he cut his way through Maddock's men like a fierce wild boar.

Tristan escaped the ambush and reached his own bed without being recognised but King Mark knew that only Tristan could have performed such a feat of arms, and again, his jealousy overwhelmed his affection. He sent Isolt to live in the stone tower which Tristan had built on the Island. For that tower was meant to defy a desperate siege, and its only entrance was ten feet above ground and reached by a ladder. He also posted thirty guards at the foot of the ladder, to see that no man entered except the King himself.

Both King Mark and Tristan were miserable without Isolt's company, and it was inevitable that one or the other would very soon yield to his desire to see her. But Tristan's need was the more urgent, for Isolt had sent Bronwen to beg him to visit her.

Tristan remembered Faithful Ronald's story of how his mother had visited his father when he was badly wounded so he dressed himself up as an old woman and walked with bent knees. Then Bronwen escorted him past all the guards and into the tower, telling everyone that he was an old witch come to heal a sickness which afflicted the Queen. Bronwen told the truth in that lie, for Tristan quickly cured the Queen's sickness and made her well with love, and the lovers laughed triumphantly to think that they had found a way round even that obstacle.

Tristan and Isolt did not laugh for long, for King Mark yielded to his desire to see Isolt at almost the same time as Tristan and, when Tristan was still with the Queen, Bronwen saw the King coming along the causeway towards the tower. Tristan had no time to get dressed, and while the guards were welcoming the King at the front of the tower, Tristan jumped from a window at the back, wearing only his loincloth. Even while King Mark was greeting his wife inside the tower, he heard a hubbub outside and from the window he saw Tristan surrounded by the guards. All the jealousy of two years of suspicion boiled up inside King Mark and he seized Isolt by the shoulders and glared into her eyes. "Tristan was here with you, wasn't he?" he demanded and, although Isolt shook her head, he read her guilt in her frightened eyes. "Bind Tristan firmly and imprison him in the chapel on Tintagel Head," the King commanded Maddock. "Place guards outside the chapel and never leave him alone. I want revenge for the eight years of friendship which he has betrayed. And let no one in or out of this tower for any reason whatever, until I send for Isolt."

Then the King strode away without a word to either Tristan or Isolt and, as he went, he tried to think of the most horrible way to put them to death for betraying his love. Even before he had reached his palace, he had decided that, as they had shared a bed unlawfully, they should now do so according to law. His slaves prepared a huge pile of driftwood on the downs near Saint Materiana's Church and his foresters made a large wattle hurdle, with iron chains for the arms and legs of two people. Then he summoned his lords to watch his revenge. Maddock took pleasure in guarding Tristan himself and tormented his prisoner by describing in detail all the preparations which were being made for the double execution. He kept Tristan bound, hands and feet together, and made him sit in his own filth in the middle of the tiny chapel and, when food was brought, he fed the prisoner on the point of his knife.

"This is your last meal on earth, Tristan," Maddock said one evening. "Tomorrow morning both you and your tender little chicken will be cooked better than this salted venison. Yes! Tomorrow I hope to hear you and Isolt sing the prettiest love song that you ever sang."

As Maddock leant forward on his knees, with the last hunk of meat on the point of his knife, he taunted Tristan again. "Here is your very last mouthful of meat, before you yourself go to the cook, dirty pig," he jeered.

Suddenly Tristan threw his weight backwards and kicked upwards with his bound feet. Tristan's feet hit Maddock in the crotch and lifted him off his knees, so that he fell forward on top of Tristan and dropped his knife. Tristan sank his teeth into Maddock's nose and banged his head on the floor, while his fingers searched for the knife. In a moment Tristan cut the thongs which bound him and stunned Maddock by smashing his head against the wall. Then he squeezed through the narrow window which looked out from the top of the cliff into empty air, and he leapt head-first into eternity.

No one saw Tristan's dive into the twilight, for Maddock was insensible and the guards outside the door of the chapel did not bother to watch the cliff because it fell sheer for more than two hundred feet below the only window. Tristan himself was numb with cold and blinded and breathless with the speed of flight, and he never knew what happened after he jumped. He came to his senses with his lungs bursting and his head full of stars, deep in the shadows of the dark green sea. Sheer instinct drove his muscles to work and he swam up towards the light. The surface of the sea heaved and seethed, as though it were boiling, and Tristan was flung about helplessly as each succeeding wave crashed and shattered on the rocks around the Island. But at last he was swept into calmer water. He crawled ashore and vomited up a bellyful of salt water. Then he followed the route which he had used when he met Isolt beside the pool. He climbed up the cliffs, and nearly numb with cold and weariness, he crept into the church, to shelter from the wind. There he found his faithful Master, praying desperately for Tristan to be saved from King Mark's vengeance.

Isolt meanwhile spent a troubled night clasped in Bronwen's arms. She imagined with horror her heroic lover's dear and delightful body being roasted like a suckling-pig for the entertainment of the cowards of Cornwall. But she was comforted, because she had heard that King Mark intended to burn her and Tristan together and she so longed to be near Tristan that she almost welcomed a shameful, painful death if she could be with him.

King Mark in his palace slept not at all, for anger and jealousy twisted his guts in knots, and hate and love warred in his heart, until he felt like bursting.

When day broke, the guards at the tower told Isolt to go with them to the King's court and those at the chapel went in, to fetch Tristan. Then there was such a shouting and a running here and there. Some guards took the news to the king, and others peered dizzily over the cliff where, they supposed, Tristan had jumped. They studied the two hundred feet of rock face below the chapel and searched the rocky shore, expecting to find Tristan's battered corpse, but he had disappeared into the air.

Isolt was already walking towards the mainland, when she heard the news. She laughed aloud, when she thought that Tristan had escaped. But later, when it became certain that Tristan had leapt over the cliff in the dark, she mourned his death. "Why did you not wait for me, my dear love?" she cried.

As she went to her trial, Isolt had no wish to save herself. She was eager only to join Tristan in death, and she hated King Mark for murdering him.

When King Mark heard the news of Tristan's suicide leap, at first he was angry that he had been deprived of his just revenge. But a moment later he was grateful that he had been spared the necessity of shedding his kinsman's blood and soon he felt sad that the handsome youth, whom he had loved so well, was smashed to pieces on the cruel rocks, or awash like an old sack in the relentless sea. The emotional shock of Tristan's death purged King Mark of his desire for revenge and he began to wonder whether after all he needed to burn Isolt.

The Cornish chiefs, who had been summoned to witness the punishment of Tristan and Isolt, saw that King Mark's face was no longer angry so the old abbot, who had conducted the proceedings against Isolt at the Christmas court, asked leave to speak on behalf of all the lords of Cornwall. "My Lord King!" he said, "By ancient custom the King may not kill without trial anyone of noble blood, unless he himself has caught that person in an open act of treason. Your chiefs have heard that the Lady Isolt was not found engaged in any treasonable act. They wish to know from your own mouth, Sire, whether you yourself found the Lord Tristan with the Queen in such circumstances that there was positively no doubt of her treason."

The King by now was willing to save Isolt and he answered calmly, "I did not myself see the Lord Tristan in the Queen's presence. I saw him, after he had been arrested in his underclothes outside the Queen's window."

"If the Lord Tristan was in his underclothes, Sire, were his clothes or sword found in the Queen's room?" "No, Lord Abbot! Nothing of his was found in the Queen's room."

After a short consultation the abbot spoke again. "With due respect, Sire, we advise you not to proceed too hastily. We cannot believe that the Lord Tristan, a warrior of royal family and proud bearing would visit the Queen in his drawers. We are inclined to believe that this is a new trick, invented to discredit the Queen and Lord Tristan, and we demand that the Lady Isolt should not be punished without trial before us, her fellow-nobles, according to custom."

"I grant your boon," the King said. "Let the Queen be brought before us at the place of execution. If she is willing to swear on Saint Materiana's tomb that she has never shared a bed with Tristan, I will forgive her and, if she is unwilling to declare her innocence, the Great Men of Cornwall may hear the evidence and may advise me on her punishment."

Even when Isolt saw the wood prepared for her burning, she declined to make a declaration about anything. "I have sworn enough oaths to be believed before now," she cried bitterly, "and I refuse to declare my innocence every time the wind wafts the stink of the cess-pits under My Lord's nose."

When the Great Men proceeded to try Isolt on a charge of treason, she still refused to speak. Nevertheless, they found insufficient evidence to support the charge and they advised the King to take his wife into his favour again. However, when King Mark began to speak, saying that he forgave her and would take her back to his bed and board, Isolt screamed at him like an angry gull, "I would rather burn than return to your bed and board, for not only are you disloyal to me with every whiff of scandal invented by your dwarf, but also you have murdered your own sister's son, the best-loved and best-feared man in Cornwall.

"Light the fire," she cried, "and make another sacrifice to that monstrous idol of disloyalty, Mark, the coward King of Cornwall! No one of his family is safe from his dishonourable doubts."

King Mark was purple in the face with rage and shame and he swore that Isolt should never again enter his house. But his councillors would not let him burn her, and he did not know what to do with her.

While King Mark sat chewing his beard in impotent fury, the crowd, which had come to see the burnings, stared timidly behind them. With a warning rattle of sticks and stones on wooden cups and bowls, a gang of lepers marched towards the King and everyone shrank away from their mutilated faces and crippled bodies.

"Come no nearer," the King commanded shrilly. "Say what you have to say from there."

"Since you don't want her, Lord, give her to us," the lepers' leader shouted. "None of us has had a woman for many years. We shall keep her busy and we shall keep her safe. Give her as common goods to the leper colony of Saint Nectan."

Isolt went white and shrank back but King Mark laughed, until the tears ran down his face. "Isolt the Fair, Isolt the Sun, she'll give a share to everyone," he mocked her.

Suddenly Isolt noticed the wooden bowl carried by the chief leper. It was the loving-cup that she had given Tristan when he pretended to be an Irish pilgrim on the shore at Cardiff. She took a deep breath, because in those days leprosy was feared more than death itself. Then she put her trust in the good omen of that bowl.

"I had rather be the common property of a leper colony which trusted me than the betrayed wife of a disloyal king," she shouted at King Mark. Boldly she took the hand of the leper chief and led the lepers away through the startled crowd.

A week later Tristan's faithful Master asked the King's leave to speak to him in private. "Sire," he said, "your wife, the Gracious Queen, Fair Isolt, has left Cornwall. The Lord Tristan was not killed, as you supposed, when he leaped from the top of Tintagel Head. He rescued the Queen from the lepers and he has taken her to her home in Ireland."

"Thank God!" said King Mark and, for the first time since he had seen Tristan near Isolt's tower on the Island, he smiled with pleasure. He was truly glad to hear that his beloved friends were safe.

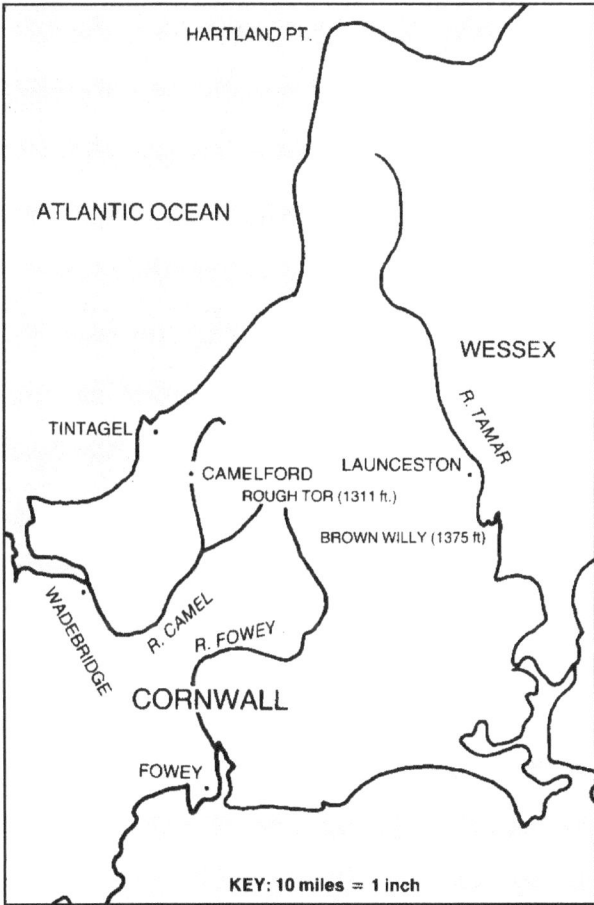

CHAPTER 17

THE CAVE

In spite of what Master had told King Mark, Tristan had not rescued Isolt from the lepers. Tristan himself had sent the dreaded outcasts to beg Isolt from the King, and he had paid them well before they went back to their colony.

Also it was untrue that Tristan and Isolt had sailed away to Ireland. They had escaped unnoticed to the barren moors inland and had made their home in a cave beneath some rocks on the top of a steep hill called Rough Tor. That was a place where few people ever came, and it was surrounded by open heathland and guarded by treacherous bogs, so that the exiled lovers felt safe from surprise. Nothing edible grew there except a few herbs but the wooded valleys at the foot of the moors were full of game, and Tristan was a great hunter.

Because of the danger of their position, living on the open moors only ten miles away from King Mark's palace, Tristan and Isolt turned night into day. The daylight hours they spent in their cave and during the night they hunted meat and gathered herbs and wood in the country around them.

In 800 A.D. even rich men lived very simply and Tristan and Isolt were not too uncomfortable living in a cavern during the summer. They had only Tristan's sword, bow and arrows to gain a living, only two blankets to cover their bed of fern, and only a harp to amuse them. But they were in love and that was their source of warmth and amusement; indeed love was their source of life.

Tristan and Isolt had lived in the cave for less than a week, when Tristan's huge hound, Huden, arrived. He had come upon his master's trail at Saint Materiana's Church and he had followed it without a rest, until he had found Tristan. Tristan and Isolt were dumb with dread, when they saw Huden, for they thought that King Mark's men might have used Huden to track them down and they also feared that, if Huden could follow their trail, another hound might do the same.

The row that Huden made! His joyful yelping, when he found his master! Tristan had to drag him inside the cave and to sit on his head, in order to silence him. "I shall have to kill him," Tristan said sadly. "If word gets round that a great hound is living on the moors, there will soon be a hunt for the hound's master."

"Don't kill our true friend," Isolt pleaded. "Be patient and try to teach him not to bay. You have often told me that after you he is the best hunter in the whole of Cornwall. With Huden to help you, perhaps we could live here even in the winter."

Tristan was delighted with Isolt's suggestion and, by tightly binding Huden's muzzle whenever he barked, he soon taught him to keep quiet in the cave. Next, Tristan took him out walking on a leash and, under threat of muzzling, he taught him not to bay when on the leash. But, whenever Tristan let him off the leash to follow a scent, he bounded over the moors in full cry and Tristan had almost given up hope of saving Huden's life, when he found a way to hunt with him.

Tristan trained Huden to work on a twenty-foot leash and he used him solely to follow a scent and to show where the game lay. Tristan himself with his bow or his sword, always killed the game but he rewarded Huden with meat from the kill so that Huden was keen to work on the leash. When managed by the leash, Huden never made a sound and he was the first of a long line of "limers" — those hounds which could follow a scent faithfully and silently on a "liam" or leash. They were the most valuable of all the hounds in a medieval hunting-pack.

The lovers lived in the cave from mid-May until early August. They had plenty of meat, because the deer were fattening up after the winter and the fawning season. Isolt found herbs to flavour their diet and Master brought bags of flour and oatmeal whenever he visited them. During the heat of the day they made music and slept, and during the twilight of morning and evening they bathed and washed their clothes in a nearby stream.

One day, when Tristan and Isolt were climbing the tor after their morning bathe, they heard not far away the hounds and horns of a large hunt. They looked at each other in alarm. This was the high season for hunting the hart, for the red deer are at their fattest and their antlers are at their finest just before the fighting and courting of the rut. Tristan and Isolt thought it probable that it was the King's own hunt which they could hear. Tristan listened carefully and judged that the hunt was only three miles away in the wooded valley of the River Camel, but he knew that men would be posted to prevent the deer escaping from the woodland up onto the open moor, and he told Isolt that there was little danger of any hunters coming near their hiding-place.

Nevertheless, the lovers were quiet and thoughtful and they did not sing or play the harp. Tristan put a boulder against the door, and when they lay down to rest, he put his sword and knife on the bed between them so that they could defend themselves if they were attacked.

King Mark had spent a miserable summer. He was very lonely, and wherever he looked he saw reminders of Tristan and Isolt. He almost forgot how they had wronged him and how he had hated them; he remembered only how much he had enjoyed their company. He missed his two friends and he behaved like a man in mourning for his nearest and dearest.

King Mark continued to act according to his royal duties and to live according to the changing seasons, but he had little interest in what he was doing. At the proper time of year his huntsmen marked where the herds of deer could be found and came to the King for instructions. When Tristan had been his companion, the King had liked hunting but now killing deer in order to feed the hundreds of people in his household was just a royal chore; he undertook it without enthusiasm.

The hunt which Tristan and Isolt had heard was indeed King Mark's. His huntsmen were drawing the woods below Camelford and the hounds startled a large herd of deer from their lodgings. Because the hunt was poorly controlled, the hunters separated and some chased one beast, some another. King Mark, with his personal kennelman and four hounds, chased a large hart with fine antlers. They followed the hart up onto the open moors, until the scent was lost at a pool in a peat bog among the high tors.

When his hounds were faulted at the water, King Mark lost interest in the chase and, because it was midday and very hot, he dismounted and rested on the grass. Meanwhile, his kennelman coupled up the hounds and led them on the leash, trying to find where the beast had left the water. Although the hounds found no scent of the hart, the man saw a faint track leading from the water towards the top of the tor and he followed it.

The kennelman found a door hidden among some rocks but he could not open it, and half curious but half afraid of fairies, he looked among the rocks for another entrance. A smoke-blackened rock led him to a hole, which served both as smoke-vent and as window to the mysterious cavern and he looked in.

In the dark cave, which was lit only by the weird green light filtering through holes partly blocked by grass, he saw two figures. He did not know whether they were gods or fairies, nor whether indeed they were alive or dead and he hurried away, with his hair bristling and his skin prickling in dread of the unknown. He had seen only that the figures were male and female and that their beauty was not of his vile world.

The huntsman told the King, and the King went to see the strange sight which had so frightened his down-to-earth servant. King Mark in his turn peered through the hole into the cavern and he saw quite clearly his once-dear friends, Tristan and Isolt, lying innocently asleep, with a sword between them like a virtuous sentry. Even ugly and evil people look pleasanter in sleep and the handsome Tristan and the beautiful Isolt looked glorious indeed. They seemed, as the kennelman had said, like a god and a goddess.

King Mark's heart turned over and over in his chest. Suddenly he loved Tristan, as he had loved him in the old days before his marriage and equally he loved Isolt, as he had loved her when she became his bride. He could hardly breathe, because he loved them so, and he was filled with a deeply sweet sadness to see his dear friends lying so lovely, so innocent, and so helpless as though entombed alive by his merciless hatred.

King Mark put some grass over the smoke-vent, to guard the lovers from other prying eyes. Then he went back to his horse and huntsman, recalled the hunt, and returned to Tintagel with hardly a word spoken. In the evening, when Tristan and Isolt awoke, they found the smoke-hole covered and they found the tracks of two men with hounds and horses. They did not know what to make of it but after that, they kept a sharp look-out for unwelcome visitors.

Two days after the hunt, Isolt, who was on watch above their cave, called to Tristan, "A party of horsemen is riding towards us from the north. There are five men, five women and two spare horses.

Come and look." Tristan and Isolt watched from their hiding-place and gripped their weapons, for the riders dismounted at the foot of the tor and a man and a woman came walking up the hill. Suddenly, with wonder in his voice, Tristan said, "It is Bronwen and Master. But I wish that they had come without an escort."

Bronwen and Master knelt respectfully to their lord and lady and then ran to embrace their friends. "He wants you back. He wants you back. He wants you back," Bronwen cried, holding Isolt's hands and dancing round her.

Tristan looked enquiringly at Master.

"Yes! It is true, Lord," Master said. "The King has sent us to invite you to return to his court. He confirms the rank and privileges which formerly belonged to you and the Gracious Queen, and promises both of you his trust and favour. He undertakes to forgive and forget any wrong which you did him and he asks very humbly that you and the Queen will forgive and forget the wrong which he did you."

"And what about the Great Men of Cornwall? What about the slanderers and the rumour-mongers of the King's court?" Tristan asked harshly.

"Lord, the invitation to you and to the Queen has been approved by the whole council of chiefs and abbots, and the King and his lords undertake to do their best to put a stop to rumours which discredit you and the Queen. Also, the traitor Maddock has been banished from the court."

"We have been happier here these past three months than ever we were in the King's court," Tristan cried. However, he squared his shoulders and added firmly, "But it is not the destiny of the sons and daughters of kings and queens to hide their honour in a cave. Gracious Lady, Fair Isolt, we have been wondering whether this cave could serve us for a home in bitter winter weather but our destiny summons us to better lodgings. Both of us were born with the honour and burden of royalty and we cannot cast it off."

"My wish is to do as you wish, Lord Tristan," Isolt answered humbly. "But I was happier here in poverty and dishonour than I can ever hope to be in riches and honour. For you are my riches, Sir and my highest honour is your love."

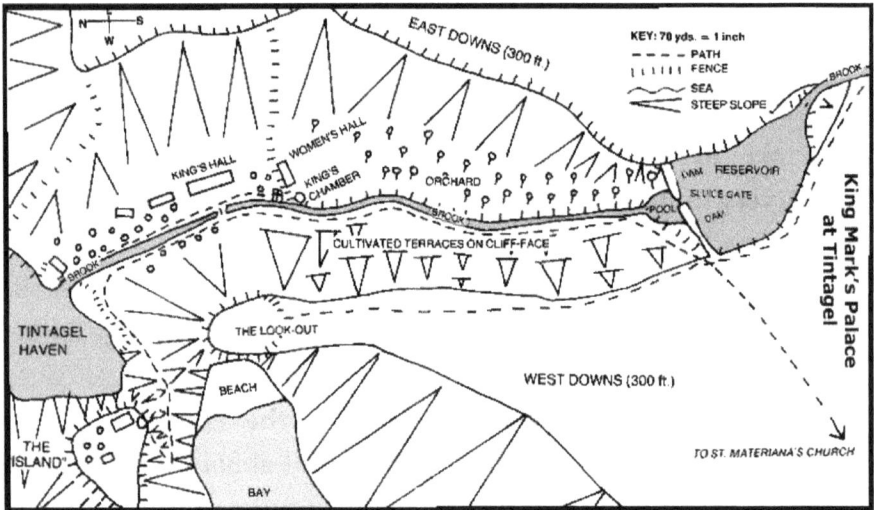

CHAPTER 18

PARTING

Tristan and Isolt were welcomed back with honour to King Mark's court, and even Mellot the King's sly jester, sang little songs and made little jokes in their honour. King Mark praised their harping and singing and he delighted in their company and conversation but he warned them clearly, 'For the love of God, dear friends, do nothing against my honour. I will shut my ears to rumours and gossip; indeed I will try to stop all backbiting in my court and I will neither test nor trap you. But, if you value my honour and your own lives, avoid open treason. For all our sakes please be discreet."

The lover's listened respectfully to the King's warning and they tried not to behave like lovers when they were in public. But for the past three months in the cave they had been as free as the air and as open as the sky in their love. It was difficult for them to refrain from the glances and caresses which lovers delight in, and it was impossible for them to refrain from the passionate act of love to which they were driven by every jangling nerve in their young bodies.

King Mark stamped firmly on all rumours that Tristan and Isolt were now, and had always been lovers, and he made no attempt to trap them in treason or to prevent their secret meetings. Indeed he made so few demands on their services that they were able to meet every day either in the women's hall or in the orchard, or on the sea-shore when Isolt went to gather medicinal seaweed. All these meetings were arranged by the experienced Bronwen, and because the lovers were intent on each other, it was Bronwen who guarded their honour and their secret meetings. Tristan, Isolt, and King Mark tried to ward off their dread of the future by enjoying the present. But, while they lived in uneasy peace at Tintagel, Maddock lived in angry exile far from court. Maddock prayed daily for vengeance on Tristan, for he blamed Tristan for his disgrace and he was jealous of him for the sake of Isolt. Through his helper Mellot, whom he paid well, Maddock was kept informed of all Tristan's movements and he waited to take his revenge when Tristan was away from the King's palace.

Maddock's chance came, when the King sent Tristan out into the countryside to gather meat for the great court at Easter. It was the fawning season for all female deer; the big harts and bucks had to be reserved for killing at their prime in high summer. Beasts, birds and men were also thin and fleshless after the sparse feeding of winter and early spring. Supplying the table for a feast in springtime was therefore difficult, so Tristan had to arrange a hundred small operations — to tease out the herds and kill three hundred young deer, to trap or shoot one thousand partridge and duck, to run down one thousand hares and rabbits, and to track down and kill all the fierce wild boar that he could find.

Maddock disguised himself as a hunt-servant and in the turmoil of the hunt he found a chance to shoot at Tristan from close range. Maddock got away without being discovered or recognised, but the wounded Tristan was carried on a hurdle to the nearest homestead. He had an arrow clean through his thigh; an artery had been pierced and he had lost much blood.

Tristan sent a message asking King Mark to send Isolt, the best doctor in Cornwall, to heal his wound. But that same day news reached Tintagel that four hundred well-armed Englishmen had landed at Wadebridge, less than fifteen miles away, and King Mark, in alarm, told Isolt and her ladies to retreat to the Island. Isolt wept and demanded to be taken to Tristan, but the distraught King sent her under guard to live in the tower.

King Mark hardly had time to send out messengers to summon his war-host, before the invaders were upon him. He rashly tried to save his palace from pillage by attacking the English with only two hundred men. As a result he lost eighty men as well as his palace, and he was besieged in his island fortress, safe himself, but helpless to save his people.

Since King Mark was cooped up on the Island, he ordered his chiefs to gather with their men under Tristan's command. But Tristan could not even put his foot to the ground. He promised to do battle when he could sit a horse, in about a week's time. Meanwhile, he advised the chiefs to avoid a pitched battle, but to harass the English and to keep them short of food and horses. He advised King Mark to gain time by bargaining with the enemy as though he wished to buy them off with gold.

For the next week the English invaders camped on the open downs to the east of King Mark's palace, for that place overlooked the palace, the haven and King Mark's fortress on the Island. They brought their ships to anchor in the haven; they blocked the causeway to the Island and they tried to prevent the Cornish skin-boats carrying food and messages to the King. As long as they hoped to win a great treasure without the trouble of fighting for it, the English preferred to remain inside their fenced camp. They hoped to starve King Mark on the Island before they themselves had eaten the stores which had been collected in his palace for the Easter feast.

When Tristan was able to ride again, he went down to the coast. Then in the night, he was rowed to the Island and climbed the cliffs to talk to King Mark. His wound reopened during the climb and he was bleeding and exhausted, when he reached the tower. Heedless of everyone else, Isolt ran to comfort him and, while Tristan talked to the King, she cleaned his wound with wine and rebandaged it with a herbal plaster.

At dawn Tristan went back to his boat, but at Isolt's insistence, instead of climbing down the cliffs, he was lowered by a line tied under his arms. The King had approved Tristan's plan of battle and had given Tristan orders for his chiefs. All the next day preparations were made and during the night the Cornish war-host advanced stealthily to Saint Materiana's Church on the downs to the west of King Mark's palace.

When dawn broke, the English sentries on the east side of the ravine in which King Mark's palace lay, shouted in warning and sounded their horns for they had seen the host of Cornwall standing in arms on the opposite side of the ravine. But, while the English were gazing westwards, trying to estimate the strength of the enemy, shouts of alarm and clouds of smoke arose from the haven, for in the dusk of dawn Tristan had led a fleet of twenty Cornish skin-boats into Tintagel haven and Cornish fishermen were setting fire to the Englishmen's wooden ships.

The English warriors on guard at the causeway between King Mark's palace and his island fortress ran down to the shore and put off in boats, hoping to save their precious ships. King Mark was then able to cross to the Lookout and join his war-host on the West Downs. The Cornishmen took heart from their King's presence and laughed at the panic on the East Downs opposite. Some of the Englishmen were running to attack the Cornish war-host and some were running to save their ships. Nevertheless, the English fought well that day. They drove the skin-boats from the haven and although the Cornish host outnumbered them by two to one, they fought it to a standstill.

At nightfall the two exhausted hosts remained almost where they had started the day. The English still held the haven and their camp on the East Downs and the Cornishmen held the Island, the Lookout and the West Downs. On one side there remained only two hundred Englishmen able to bear arms, with only two ships afloat. On the other side, only four hundred Cornishmen were fit to fight again.

When the next day dawned, the leaders of both sides encouraged their men to renew the battle but the men were too weary and too sore. So the two hosts lay all day, looking at each other across the ravine of the King's palace. Men from both sides came to the reservoir for water, but some stones and arrows flying across the valley were all the greetings which they gave each other. Food and ale were scarce on both sides and there was much talk of retreating in the night. But King Mark and the English Elderman both knew that the host which turned its back was doomed, not only to defeat, but also to destruction, so each urged his men to stand fast through the night.

The next morning the English Elderman found his men still unwilling to fight but he knew that he could not get home to Wessex without a battle. Therefore he strode to the edge of the ravine and shouted across it: "Ho there, men of Cornwall! We have fought well and both sides have had very heavy losses. It would be a pity if more good men were killed unnecessarily. Therefore send a champion to fight with me and let us decide in single combat which side shall keep the field, and which side shall depart empty-handed."

When this message was brought to King Mark, he summoned his chiefs and asked their advice but, whatever he said, he could not persuade them either to name a champion or to fight another battle. They said only that they wanted to go home. Tristan was there beside the King, lying on a mattress, dark-eyed and pale, his right leg bandaged from the groin to the knee. "By Saint Michael and the host of Heaven, dear friends, do not give up the contest, when the war is almost won," Tristan cried. "The Elderman's challenge is not a sign of strength; it is a sign of weakness. His men have refused to leave camp to fight but he knows that, if they wait much longer, they will all starve and he knows that, if they try to walk back to Wessex without first routing you, they will all be killed or captured before they reach the River Tamar. For God's sake and your own honour, Lords, even if you cannot find a champion to fight the Elderman Alfick, at least stand fast."

"No! We want to go home," the Cornish chiefs said. "Unless you, Lord Tristan, will fight the Elderman, we shall go home tonight."

"By Saint Michael and the heavenly host!" Tristan shouted angrily. "I have already suffered too much on your behalf. How often have I fought, to save you and your sons and your feeble honour? And how often have I been wounded by your slanders and spite? See! Here I lie, struck down by a traitorous Cornish arrow and yet you ask me to kill myself for your sakes.

"By my cunning and advice, I have given you the means of victory. For the love of God, men of Cornwall, stretch out your hands and take it" Tristan pleaded. "For the honour of your King and country, for your own good names, my friends, stand fast, until these Englishmen admit defeat. I promise you that there will be rich booty when they start out on their long walk home, and there will also be strong slaves to be won at the end of it."

For all Tristan's pleading the Cornish chiefs stuck to their decision. "We shall go home, unless you fight the Elderman Alfick," they insisted.

"Tristan!" King Mark cried. "You are my sister's child and my son by adoption, and unless the Lady Isolt gives me a son, you will be the heir to both my treasure and my kingdom. For your own sake as well as mine," he pleaded, "save us in this time of trouble. If the English are masters of the field of battle, all the treasure looted from my palace will be removed to Wessex, and I shall be a fugitive wandering the hills to escape the conquerors. The Kingdom of Cornwall will be lost forever and the men of Cornwall will become the slaves of English masters."

"Lord King, I do not lack the heart to fight; I lack the strength," Tristan replied tartly. "Weak and limping as I am, how could I defeat the great Elderman Alfick? If I fought him, I should lose my life and you would lose the war because of my failure."

But King Mark argued, "If you fight Alfick, you may defeat him by your cunning and skill, but if you do not fight, my war-host will desert me and I shall certainly lose my kingdom and my treasure."

Then the King and all the chiefs of Cornwall knelt around Tristan's bed and begged him to be their champion once again. The chiefs promised with sacred oaths to accept him willingly as the King's heir presumptive and never to say a word against him.

But Tristan still refused, until King Mark cried, 'For my sweet Queen's sake, Tristan, do not let the English drive us into the hills. For the love of Isolt, do not let her become a landless fugitive or an English slave."

"I consent, My Lord!" Tristan said then. "If the men of Cornwall will stand fast for the rest of the day, I will fight the Elderman Alfick for the Queen's sake. But I rely on you to keep the Elderman on his feet, while I eat and sleep in the cool of the church."

During the heat of the day, the Cornishmen stood armed on the western side of the dividing valley. They pretended to be eager to attack the English and they kept the Elderman waiting in full armour for the Cornish champion who, they said, would soon arrive to fight him.

At midday Tristan sent Master to agree with the Elderman the place for the combat. Master argued so long that at last the Elderman reluctantly consented to fight on the earth bank which dammed the valley to create a reservoir. Impatiently the Elderman waited among his thanes at the eastern end of the dam and ever more furiously he demanded the arrival of the Cornish champion. Meanwhile, Tristan ate well and slept for two hours in the quiet church.

When the church bell sounded for None, the mid-afternoon service, the Elderman saw a litter being carried through the Cornish host towards the reservoir. The litter was set down and Tristan stepped out, lazily yawning and stretching his arms to show his contempt for his opponent. Tristan's mail byrnie hid the heavy bandaging around his right thigh, but he found it difficult to climb down to the dam without showing his limp.

The two champions advanced along the dam. They were alone in the valley, with the two war-hosts looking down on them from either side of the ravine. On one side of the dam there lay the deep water of the reservoir full of the winter's rain, and on the other side there was a steep drop from the earth wall to a deep pool in the valley bottom.

Tristan had insisted on fighting on the dam, because its top was only four feet wide, for he did not want to have to circle around on his stiff leg. But there was one particular disadvantage about fighting on the dam. At its mid-point there was a sluice-gate for controlling the outflow of water, and the bridge over the waterfall was simply a wooden plank which was six feet long but only one foot wide.

Tristan knew that his feeble strength would not endure for long and he crossed the plank before the fight began, in the hope of forcing an early decision. But Alfick was a wily fighter, and as soon as Tristan had crossed the plank, Alfick attacked fiercely and tried to push Tristan backwards into the sluice. Tristan had to summon up all his strength in order to resist Alfick's rush, and with the effort his wound reopened.

Alfick soon noticed the red bloodstain on Tristan's trousers and he began to jeer and to press his attack. But Tristan, with the narrow plank over the rushing waterfall close behind his heels, defended doggedly and saved his failing strength. The English cheered to see the battle so one-sided but the Cornishmen groaned, when they saw Tristan weary, bleeding and unable to strike a blow. Some Cornish chiefs called for their horses and made ready to depart.

Tristan was tired but not so tired as he pretended, and although his spear drooped low, he held it low on purpose. When Alfick hurled his spearpoint at Tristan's head, Tristan ducked under the blow and, while Alfick was stretched forward in drawing back his spear, Tristan thrust his spear under Alfick's shield and byrnie, and right through the meat of Alfick's left thigh. Then at once he dropped the spear shaft. Alfick stumbled, with the heavy spear dragging at his leg, and retreated a few paces to pull the spear out. But Tristan turned and hurried across the plank, then faced his enemy from beyond the rushing water.

The champions faced each other across the six foot gap, bridged only by a single slippery plank. Each held his round shield before his face but only Alfick now had a spear. Tristan had lost his spear for the sake of crossing the bridge, but he drew his sword to meet Alfick's attack.

Alfick also unsheathed his sword and put it into his left hand behind his shield. Then he drew his spear back behind his shoulder and flung it with all his might. Tristan could not avoid the winging spear and he took it on his shield but the sharp blade bit deep into the wood and the nine-foot-long shaft dragged heavily on Tristan's shield-arm.

Alfick, having flung his spear, took his sword in his right hand and limped across the plank with his shield before him and sword raised to strike. But Tristan threw his shield, with Alfick's spear still stuck in it, at Alfick's feet, and as Alfick stumbled on the bouncing plank, Tristan swung his sword with two hands like a scythe and swept Alfick off the plank into the pool below the waterfall. In order to save himself from drowning in the turbulent water, Alfick had to drop his sword and shield, and before he could climb out of the water, Tristan was standing over him.

"Yield yourself defeated, Elderman Alfick," Tristan demanded. But Alfick, though nearly drowned by his heavy armour, only looked around him for a chance of escape. "Englishmen!" Tristan shouted to the Wessex thanes who were watching from the side of the valley. "Will you admit defeat, so that I can spare your brave Elderman's life? Or must I kill him, to prove that Cornwall has won both the field and the spoils of battle?"

"What terms do you propose, Champion of Cornwall?" the English thanes asked.

"Every man may take himself safely back to Wessex, with his helmet and byrnie, his sword and shield only. But your ships and horses, your long spears and axes, all your belongings and all your spoils you must leave unharmed in your camp."

The terms were acceptable and Tristan let Alfick go, to lead the long march home to Wessex. But the Cornish chiefs, who had done so little to gain the victory, treacherously attacked the weary English on their march. The English were on foot, without spears or axes and without shelter, and the mounted Cornish bowmen and slingers eventually killed or captured all of them. The Elderman Alfick died but with his last breath he cursed and reviled the cowardly Cornishmen who so soon broke their champion's word. When Tristan heard how his word and honour had been betrayed, he had his bed carried into the King's hall and cursed all Cornishmen from King to cowman.

The Cornish chiefs hated Tristan for his excellence and after only a few months they broke their promise to accept him willingly as the King's heir. They bribed Mellot, the jester, to trick King Mark into finding Tristan in an act of open treason. One sunny day, when Mellot knew that Tristan had gone to visit the Queen, he told King Mark some news from Ireland and he advised the King to ask the Queen's opinion, since she was Irish.

But the King was afraid of what he might find if he visited the Queen's quarters without warning. "Where is the Lord Tristan?" he asked and added as explanation, "Tristan knows as much about Ireland as the Queen. I should like to ask his advice first."

"I saw the Lord Tristan ride out hunting, Sire," Mellot lied. "If you want to consult him, you will have to wait until this evening."

"Then I must ask the Queen," King Mark said, and believing that he could visit her without fear of finding Tristan with her, he went into the orchard behind the women's hall. The Queen's ladies were taken by surprise and the King came upon his wife lying under the trees, asleep in Tristan's arms.

King Mark started back with the shock of it. He was almost choked with horror and jealousy. But, when he saw the triumphant smile on Mellot's face, he took him by the throat and squeezed until his rage was spent. "You at least shall not see my dear friends burn, you poisonous dwarf," he muttered, as he dropped him dead into the stream. "But I cannot ignore this open treason" he said sadly. "If the Abbot sees them like that, he will want to light the fire himself."

The King went to fetch his councillors but some hunter's instinct had woken Tristan and he had seen the King looking at him. As soon as the King went away, therefore, Tristan awakened Isolt and told her, "Lady, today is the death-day of our love, for I must leave you. The King himself has seen us together and he has gone to fetch witnesses. If his witnesses find me here with you, he will have us burned, but if his witnesses find you alone and asleep, you will be safe.

"So long as I remain in Cornwall, I shall be a danger to you and I had rather be sad without you than be the cause of your dishonour and death. Therefore I must sail away. But never forget me, Lady; and kiss me now for remembrance sake."

"My own Lord!" Isolt answered; "I have been yours so completely and for so long, that even if you were dead, I could never forget you. Promise me, Lord Tristan, that you will never let any other woman be as close to you as I have been, and take this ring to remind you of me. By this ring, and this only, I shall recognise any messenger from you. If a messenger claiming to come from you cannot show me this ring, I shall know that he is false, but if he shows the ring, I will do whatever he asks. Yes! I will do your will even at the risk of my own death or disgrace. In return, Sire, please leave with me our loyal friend, your hound Huden, for he shared our happiest days and I will cherish him for the sake of those days, when you are far away."

Tristan kissed Isolt and slipped away unseen and, as he had said, when the King's councillors found Isolt alone and apparently asleep, they reproached the King for unworthy suspicions. Although Isolt escaped death and dishonour, she was stunned by the sudden shock of her lover's departure. She sat on her bed, dry-eyed, silent and staring like a fool, until Bronwen led her up onto Tintagel Head to watch Tristan's ship sail into the sunset.

Then Isolt shrieked with the pain of parting and she cried over the sea: "Ah, my love! I suffer now ten times more than if I was being torn apart by wild horses, for my living heart is sailing away with you and my body, which remains here, is only a lifeless shell.

"If you had remained, Tristan, you would by now be both dead and dishonoured. Therefore stay away from me and preserve your life and your high honour. Keep alive for my sake, noble Tristan and most reluctantly, I shall keep alive for your sake."

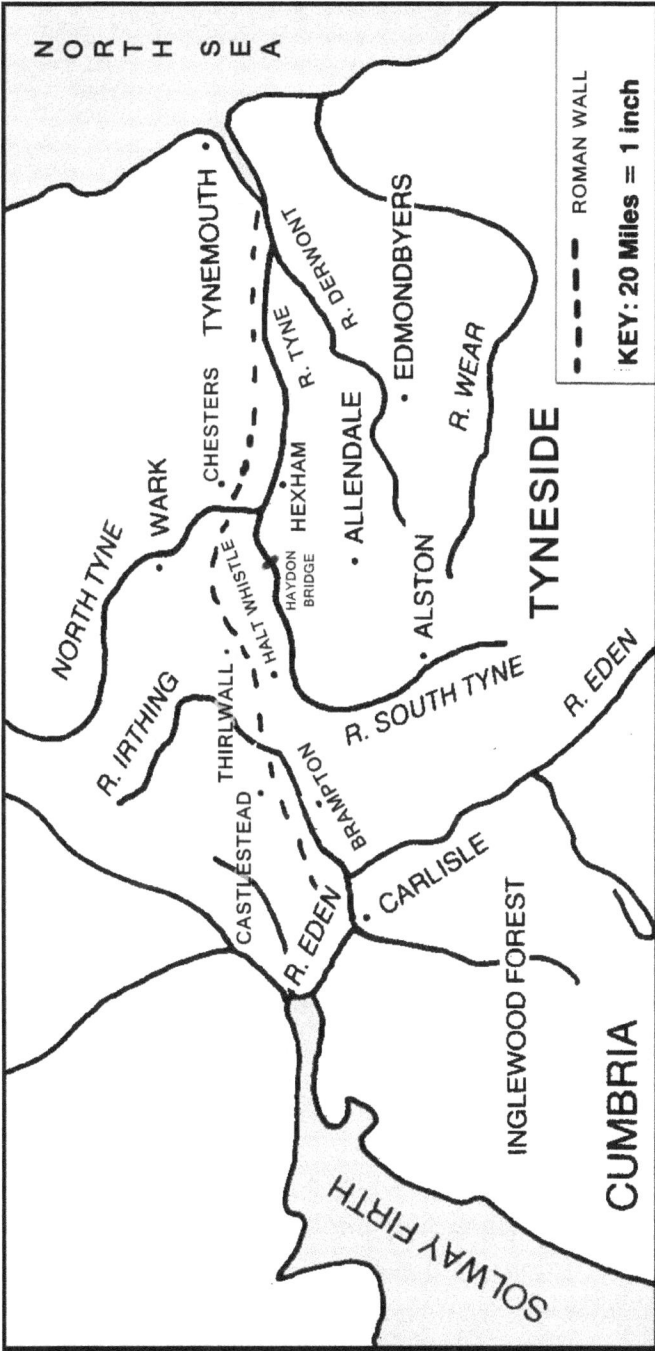

CHAPTER 19

THE OTHER ISOLT

Tristan tried to bury his grief in the search for honour and a warrior's fame. He tried to forget his heart's death by seeking his body's death, for he found that only in the mortal crunch of war could he forget his lover for a while. From Cornwall, Tristan sailed to Normandy and he took service under the great Charles, King of the Franks, who was preparing for a new war in Italy. When that war and the imperial crown had been won, Charlemagne wanted to keep Tristan with him in his peacetime court, for Tristan had gathered great fame. But Tristan could not bear the aching love-longing which tormented him whenever he was at leisure, and after one winter of enforced idleness he sailed back to his childhood home, Lothian.

Tristan's foster-parents, the Marshal Ronald and the Lady Florence were dead, but his foster-brothers welcomed him as their lord and they offered to give him back the lands and titles which he had renounced six years before. But Tristan was content with the overlordship which was still his and he had no wish to settle down to rule a kingdom.

Tristan found that Ronald's sons had strengthened the boundaries of Lothian against the English of Northumbria and were at peace. But he was told that Cumbria - the southern part of the old British kingdom of Strathclyde - was at war with Northumbria and war was what Tristan wanted. Therefore, he rode over the hills to Carlisle, to aid the King of Cumbria. There he was welcomed with great honour, because his fighting fame was known to everybody in Celtic Britain and Ireland. The King of Cumbria's son, an eager young warrior called Cardin, was particularly friendly towards Tristan and he told Tristan about the war.

"For many years the English of Northumbria have been nibbling at our frontiers, driving our beasts to their stockades and feeding their cattle on our pastures" Cardin told Tristan. "And three sharp thorns are forever pricking our tender flesh, — the thanes Wulf of Wark, Halfdan of Hexham and Ulf of Allendale. Every summer those thanes raid and burn westward along the valley of the River South Tyne, and over the fells on either side of it. They boast that they can camp on the banks of our River Eden any time that they choose."

"If your father, the King, would accept my help, friend Cardin," Tristan said, "I should very much like to pull some hairs out of those three thanes' beards. For the English are my favourite enemies. I have fought them both in Lothian and in Cornwall, and once I killed the Northumbrian king in his own hall. I can truthfully boast that I know their style. They are strong men and fierce fighters but they are slow movers across country and very easily deceived."

Cardin persuaded the King to summon his war-host for a campaign against the English and Tristan asked his foster-brothers to send him as many mounted warriors as they could spare from Lothian. The English heard of the gathering of the war-host of Cumbria and they scorned it, for they had often beaten it. But Tristan hid the five hundred men who rode over from Lothian in the stone forts at Castlesteads and Thirlwall on Hadrian's old Roman wall; and their arrival was not known in Northumbria.

In the warm darkness of a summer night, Tristan and Cardin led one hundred Cumbrian warriors along the Roman wall to Chesters, and from there, in the first light of day, they rode down to the gates of Hexham. They shot flaming arrows into the thatched roofs of the English homestead. "Good morning, Thane Halfdan!" they shouted.

The Cumbrians rode back up the valley of the Tyne, killing every Englishman and burning every house which they passed. As Tristan had expected, the thanes of Hexham, Wark, and Allendale, angrily summoned their men from their homesteads to gather at Haydon Bridge. They swore to ravage Cumbria to the River Eden and to camp within sight of the King's palace in Carlisle.

Halfdan of Hexham soon gathered his men, and while Ulf and Wulf waited at Haydon Bridge for the last of their men, Halfdan, with a hundred and fifty followers, rode after the raiders. Halfdan had been woken by Cumbrian hunting-horns sounding at his very gates and he wanted revenge. He galloped furiously up the South Tyne valley, a deep, wooded cleft between high, bare fells on either side but he never saw the enemy until sunset when he reached Halt Whistle. Tristan and his friends had waited there, to give Halfdan a sight of them and the English followed them to the pass over Hartleyburn Common.

In the narrow, winding pass Tristan and Cardin blocked Halfdan's way, and after a skirmish in the treacherous dusk, Halfdan made camp for the night in order to wait for his friends. The next morning the English host, by the Hartley Burn, numbered four hundred but Tristan had retreated towards Carlisle and he had sent messengers to his men in Castlesteads and Thirlwall forts, and to the King in Carlisle. The English rode confidently down into the rich lowlands but two hundred Lothian warriors from Thirlwall fort shut the pass behind them, and three hundred from Castlesteads joined Tristan and Cardin near Brampton, where they meant to give battle.

The English dismounted joyfully when they saw the warriors of Cumbria and Lothian waiting for them, and they charged forward in three howling mobs, each mob following one of the three thanes.

On Tristan's instructions, the Cumbrian slingers and mounted archers swung wide and attacked the English footmen from the flanks, but Tristan and the well-armed men of Lothian met the enemy hand to hand. The battle was indecisive for an hour or more, but then the King and his men from Carlisle joined the fight and the English began to falter.

Tristan attacked in turn each of the three standards of the three English thanes. First Halfdan was killed and the men of Hexham carried his body away for burial in his own church. Then Ulf was badly wounded and told his men to take him home. The last of the three thanes, Wulf, was killed outright by an arrow in the throat. Before evening the whole host of the Tyneside English was in flight, hurrying to reach the Hartley Burn; but two hundred Lothian warriors were waiting in the pass and very few of the four hundred Englishmen who had set out from Haydon Bridge the previous day ever returned home.

The victors searched the battlefield for booty and stripped the English dead of everything valuable. The living they examined as potential slaves but they very soon killed those who seemed unlikely to become fit for heavy work. The victorious warriors drove their prisoners and carried their loot away, to celebrate with feasting in the King's hall. Then the peasants came out to take whatever was left. Last of all came the monks with their candles and their crosses and they gave the church's last rites to any wounded man who still clung to life, and buried the dead in a large, shallow pit.

The victory feast had hardly begun, when Tristan suddenly fell silent at the board. "By Saint Michael and all the host of Heaven, good Cardin!" he burst out. "Why are we sitting here, when we should be fetching the cattle and the women from Hexham, Wark and Allendale? We shall have lost half the profit from spending so much sweat and blood, if we do not hurry to harvest the belongings of those whom we killed. Rouse your men before they are too drunk and ask the King to lead us in a hunt for Northumbrian treasure."

For a fortnight, from Haydon Bridge down to Tynemouth, the Cumbrians killed every armed Englishman whom they could catch. They gathered a vast booty of farm beasts and tools and strong young slaves and they burned or destroyed everything which they did not want, or could not carry, — buildings and boats, standing crops and stored grain, old men and cripples. The King of Cumbria cleared his frontier so thoroughly that he felt revenged for all the English raids which he had endured, and he felt safe for many years to come. He rewarded Tristan and the Lothian warriors with rich gifts in addition to their share of the booty, and when the Lothian men rode home over the hills, the King invited Tristan to remain in his court.

Tristan stayed at Carlisle but he stayed there not for the King's favour, nor for the comforts of a rich man's palace, nor for the friendship of Cardin, the King's heir. He stayed for the sake of the King's daughter. But it was not because she was beautiful, which she was, nor because she was clever, charming and unmarried, which also she was. He was attracted to her principally because she was named Isolt, Isolt Whitehands.

For two long years Tristan had been remembering and dreaming about his lover, Isolt Fairhair, the Queen of Cornwall but he could not speak of her, for fear of bringing her into disrepute. Now he had found an Isolt whom he could name openly and in whose honour he could compose songs and all the loving words which he wanted to whisper about Isolt Fairhair, he cried aloud about Isolt Whitehands. If Tristan had not been so completely obsessed by his passionate thoughts of Isolt Fairhair, he would have realised what people would think of his continual praising of Isolt Whitehands. Both the girl herself and her family and friends were convinced that Tristan praised her because he admired her.

Cardin was pleased to see his new friend interested in his sister and he persuaded the King that it would be a good thing for Cumbria if the mighty Tristan could be induced to marry and settle down with them. Cardin therefore fostered the friendship between Tristan and Isolt Whitehands and he often took Tristan to the women's hall, to play the harp for Isolt and to talk with her. Isolt herself was both flattered by the admiration of so famous a warrior prince and attracted by his good looks and courtly skills so she encouraged him by making it clear that she enjoyed his company.

As often happens, Tristan's make-believe began to take on the substance of reality and his songs about Isolt, though inspired by his love for the Queen of Cornwall, persuaded him that the King of Cumbria's daughter also deserved his praise. Tristan advanced from stage to stage in his courting of Isolt Whitehands, tangling glances, touching hands, weaving hidden messages into ordinary conversation, and however eagerly he approached her, she was always just as eager as he was. The very warmth of her affection for him kindled his passion and he who had sworn to be true to Isolt Fairhair now found himself desiring Isolt Whitehands.

Tristan reproached himself. He reminded himself of his promise to Isolt the Fair and he reminded himself that she had never swerved from her devotion to him. After this reprimand Tristan was overwhelmed by memories of his lover. He sat by Isolt Whitehands and sighed; he stood beside her and stared and often in her presence he muttered and moped with melancholy. Everyone could see that Tristan was pining with unsolaced love and they all assumed that he pined for the favours of Isolt Whitehands.

When Isolt Whitehands saw Tristan pining, the fire of her own love was fanned into flames, and she too began to sigh and to change colour, to eat little and to sleep badly, to be miserable out of his company and melancholy in it. Tristan realised what had happened and he tried to amuse her and to distract her from her thoughts of love. He used all his skills of music and conversation to entertain her, but the more and the better he performed, the more and the better she loved him.

The more fiercely Isolt loved Tristan, the more her looks scorched him and the more her touch made him tingle. Soon Tristan caught fire from the passionate girl; his body burned for hers, as her body burned for his. He began to excuse himself: *If I am ever to escape from the stranglehold of my doomed love for Isolt the Fair, it can only be through a new love affair. If I can bring myself to love this Isolt, perhaps my love for the other Isolt will die.*

When Tristan thought of killing his love for Isolt Fairhair by loving Isolt Whitehands, he began to wonder whether Isolt Fairhair had already forgotten him. *For,* he told himself: *no message from her has ever reached me. Perhaps she is happy with her lord, King Mark, and has no more need of me. Truly our fate is uneven, for Isolt the Fair has a husband in her bed, while I lie always alone. I do not know if she can still love me in spite of the comfort which she gets from Mark but, by the host of Heaven, I mean to find out. This Cumbrian girl is throwing herself at me. So I will marry her and find out for myself how it feels to be in love with one woman and wedded to another. Perhaps my love-longing will be less painful and I may even be cured of it.*

In this frame of mind Tristan asked the King for his daughter's hand, and since the marriage pleased everyone, it was soon arranged. Tristan was married to Isolt Whitehands in the cathedral porch in the sight of all the Great Men of Cumbria and, after the Nuptial Mass, the wedding feast and the afternoon sports, it came time for supper and then for bed. Tristan had planned that the bridal bed should be the foundation of his marriage to Isolt Whitehands, for he argued that, as Isolt Fairhair had a husband to cure the fevers of her body, so he, Tristan, ought to have a wife to cool his passion. But on this very point his plans went astray.

Cardin and the friends who undressed Tristan smiled at his eagerness to join the bare bride waiting in his bed. But suddenly, in pulling the sleeve from Tristan's arm, they pulled a ring from his finger. The ring clattered and rolled across the floor. Tristan stared at it and went as pale as death. It was the ring which Isolt Fairhair had given him when he left her. He remembered his promise that he would never let any other woman be as close to him as she had been and yet he now saw himself about to celebrate the central act of love with another woman.

Tristan crept into bed with his hand on his heart and, when his bride kissed his lips and eyes and held him close to her eager body, he groaned. "Dear wife!" he said: "Please excuse me from love-play tonight. I have an old wound, which is troubling me and I dare not tire myself, when I have this pain, for it often brings on dizziness and vomiting."

"My Lord, I am far more sad for your pain than I am for missing one night's love-play" his bride answered kindly. "But on both counts I hope that you will soon be well."

Tristan lay in torment. He was burning with shame for having betrayed his absent lover by marrying but he was burning with desire for the passionate girl who lay warm and naked by his side. He could not dishonour his newly wedded bride by leaving her bed but he would not betray his old lover by making love to his wife.

Tristan knew that his wife burned as hot as he did; he knew that she was as eager as he was to quench the flames and he knew that, when those flames had once been quenched, she would eagerly fan them into throbbing life again. He knew that, unless he satisfied her, her hot desire would turn at last to hotter hate. But the torment of his baffled body and the danger of a jealous wife he accepted, almost welcomed, as his penance for betraying his old love, and Isolt Whitehands remained a virgin.

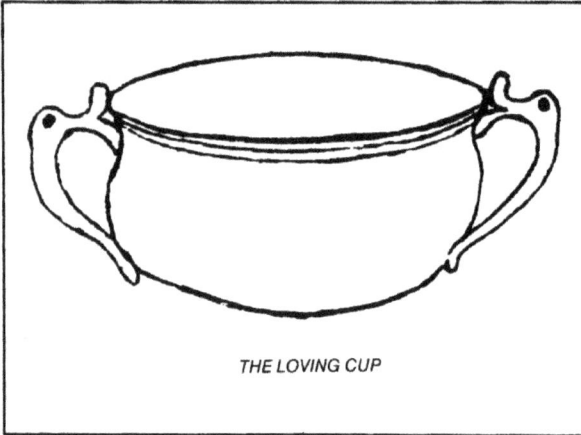

THE LOVING CUP

CHAPTER 20

DESPERATE DEVICES

Tristan lived with his wife in the King's palace in Carlisle throughout the winter. She was still a virgin but he praised Isolt as keenly as before and, although her body was far from satisfied, her heart was at ease, because he said so often that he loved Isolt more than his life. Isolt Whitehands trusted Tristan and, since she knew that he visited no other woman, she was content to wait, until he was well enough to make love to her.

On the Feast of Candlemas (second of February) Tristan and his wife went with Cardin to Saint Ninian's shrine at Brampton, for, to ensure a good harvest in the coming summer, it was necessary to honour Cumbria's patron saint at the beginning of spring. Isolt was riding beside her brother and it happened that, as they were fording a stream called Bold Water, her horse took fright. Isolt was a good rider and she was in no danger but the struggle to control her horse disarranged her clothes and ice-cold water splashed her warm thigh.

"Oh!" she cried in surprise but soon began to smile and, although she tried to control herself, she could not suppress her giggles of amusement. Cardin stared at her but she kept quiet and he supposed that she was laughing at him. He asked her sharply what she was laughing at and when she said nothing, he grew angry. Then at last she whispered, "I was laughing because that stream is well named 'Bold Water'. When my horse took fright, 'Bold Water' came higher up my thighs than ever I was touched by any man, even by my own husband."

Cardin was astonished. "Do you mean to say that you are still a virgin after four months of marriage? Then what does Tristan do in bed?" he asked.

"He just kisses me but never does any more. He says he has an injury."

"Injury!" Cardin exclaimed. "By Saint Ninian, Tristan injures and insults both you and your family. Either he is going after some other woman; or else he scorns us so arrogantly that he has decided not to get himself an heir of our blood."

Isolt Whitehands persuaded her brother not to mention the matter to anyone, because, she said, in everything else Tristan treated her well and she was content. But Tristan soon noticed that his friend Cardin was looking at him sourly and he asked why. Cardin told him the story of the "Bold Water" and accused him of insulting his wife and her family. Then at last Tristan was forced to explain his secret difficulty.

"Truly I had hoped," he said, "that your sweet sister would bring me comfort but I love another lady, who is far more fair, far more elegant and far more talented than your sister and, after enjoying the favours of such a paragon, I cannot bring myself to make love to your sister."

"But my sister is the most beautiful, the most elegant and the most talented lady in the whole of Cumbria— as well as the best-born. By God's blood, I have a mind to kill you for so insulting her."

"Good Cardin, you are the King's heir and I am only a stranger. You could kill me without fear of revenge but by our firm friendship and by the close ties of our companionship in arms, I promise you that I do not mean to insult either you or your sister. Isolt Whitehands is sweet and beautiful, well-born and rich, but my lover is the fairest woman in the whole world. My lady is beyond compare."

"You are a liar and a cheat. You are trying to hide some foul offence beneath your lying tale. Show me this paragon; or I shall declare a feud against you," Cardin threatened.

"That will not be easy, for my lady lives in another land and is the wife of a rich and powerful man. But I want nothing so much as to see her, and if you will swear to guard my secret with your life, I will show you the world's most beautiful creature. I will show you also my lady's companion, who is as much more lovely than your sister as my lady is lovelier than her companion."

The two princes pretended to go on a pilgrimage and they put to sea wearing pilgrim's robes and escorted only by two trusted squires. But in their chests they had packed their fine clothes and their arms and armour, for their pilgrimage was not to the holy places but to the shrine of Love, and Tristan had so inflamed Cardin by describing Bronwen, that Cardin was almost as eager to see Bronwen as Tristan to see Isolt.

When the pilgrims landed in Cornwall, they asked for news of the King's court. By good luck they heard that the King, the Queen and their households were on that very day expected to pass nearby on the road to Launceston. Tristan took Cardin to a place where they could watch the road without being seen and he promised that Cardin would soon see the two loveliest women in the world.

They saw a great cavalcade kicking up the dust on the road from Tintagel. Hundreds of servants, horses and hounds, warriors and courtiers went past the pilgrims and then the King himself went by, with Maddock at his side. "But where are the ladies?" Cardin asked anxiously.

Tristan pointed back towards Tintagel. There another dust-cloud hung above the road and the Queen's household soon came into sight. This procession was led by huntsmen and kennelmen with hounds on the leash, messengers and stable-boys, with war-horses, hunters, baggage-mules and palfreys all led by the right hand and with hawks and falcons carried on the left wrist. Cardin was so impressed by the outdoor servants of the Queen's household that, when he saw a company of women, he cried, "Look! Here come the Queen and her ladies-in-waiting." But Tristan laughed at him. "Those are the laundresses and the maid-servants, who make beds and mend clothes and wash the ladies' hair," he explained.

The road was now full of the Queen's indoor staff, her ushers and chamberlains and after them came her pages and squires and attendant courtiers, singing and playing music as they rode along. After the gentlemen, came the ladies-in-waiting, the well-born and beautiful Irish girls whom Isolt had brought with her to Cornwall. Last of all, rode Isolt and Bronwen, with Huden on a gold chain.

"By Saint Ninian, Tristan!" Cardin whispered. "If these two goddesses are your lady and her companion, you have convinced me that my sister is less fair than they are. How can I speak to them?"

"Ask the Queen to guide you to some safe lodging along this road, and while you are talking, stroke her dog with my gold ring upon your hand. When she sees that ring, she will, by some means, arrange a meeting."

Cardin, still dressed in his pilgrim's clothes, bowed low to the Queen. "Please advise me, Gracious Lady, where my friend and I can spend the night. We have come from abroad and we do not know how the land lies here."

Isolt the Fair was always kind to pilgrims in memory of that pilgrim who had helped her with her oath at Cardiff and she stopped her horse to greeted Cardin. Then he put out his hand and stroked Huden. When Isolt saw the ring on his finger and understood the meaning of his innocent request, she sucked in her breath and went very pale, for she had not heard from her lover Tristan for nearly three years. The shock of it made her feel faint and she had difficulty in keeping her saddle.

"I should very much like to see your friend," she said at last. "But I cannot wait here for him. If he seeks my alms, tell him to follow us to the next house on the road. The King and his men will be sleeping inside the stockade but this lady and I will sleep in a tent in the orchard outside."

Isolt and Bronwen rode on and Cardin stood, rooted to the ground, staring after them. He thought that Bronwen was by far more beautiful than Tristan had described and he had fallen in love at first sight. As Isolt rode on, she stroked Huden's coat where Tristan's ring had touched it and her body trembled with urgent love-longing, to think of her lover coming in the night.

Both supper and bed had been prepared for the King and Queen in the hall of the house where they had planned to spend the night but after supper Isolt pretended to be ill with an itchy rash and she said that she would sleep in the orchard so as not to infect or disturb the King. A tent was pitched in a quiet place, well-protected by trees; the tent's inner walls were hung with embroidery and splendid beds were made up for the Queen and her principal lady. The Queen gave orders that, if two pilgrims arrived and asked for alms, they were to be allowed to come to her tent, but everyone else must be kept away.

Tristan and Cardin put on their best tunics and their mail byrnies under their pilgrim's robes and they rode to a wood near the King's camp. They told their squires to wait in the wood with their horses and their spears and shields but they themselves, humbly like poor beggars, walked to the orchard. Tristan asked the sentry to give the Queen a leather pouch containing his ring, and very soon they were led to her tent.

Tristan and Cardin knelt outside the tent, until Isolt and Bronwen called them in to receive their alms and greeted them with hugs and kisses. While Tristan and Isolt told each other their news and confirmed their love, Cardin courted Bronwen. He offered her his service in return for her favour and, when Tristan and Isolt went to Isolt's bed, Cardin persuaded Bronwen to share her bed with him. But Bronwen was unwilling to be won so quickly and she drugged Cardin's wine, so that he slept the whole night through.

The next day Isolt feigned sickness and would not leave her tent and the four lovers spent the whole day in courting and games. But in the evening, just when Cardin had hoped to make love to Bronwen, she tricked him again and put him to sleep. In the morning, when Isolt teased Cardin for being a sleepy lover, he found it difficult not to be sulky. Tristan and Isolt were so happy that they could not bear to see Cardin unhappy and they begged Bronwen to give Cardin his desire. Isolt praised him lavishly and Tristan declared that he was the bravest warrior in the north of Britain. Therefore on the third night Bronwen allowed Cardin to woo her in the darkness and all four left their sleep to catch up later.

When the Queen's sickness continued into the third day, Maddock persuaded the King to continue his journey to Launceston and he promised to guard the Queen himself and to bring her along as soon as she was well. But Maddock was hoping to gain the Queen's love. He reasoned that, if she had needed a lover when the King was younger, she must need a lover even more now, for the King was growing old and Tristan had been gone a long time. He therefore went to spy on the Queen.

Maddock circled the orchard where Isolt had her tent, and by chance, he came upon the squires and horses of Tristan and Cardin, hidden in the wood. The squires slung the princes' shields upon their backs and put their helmets on their heads and carried their spears in their hands, then they galloped away, in spite of Maddock's threats and challenges. In the Queen's tent Tristan and Cardin heard the noise and heeded the warning so they escaped on foot without being seen. Later, when the two princes found their squires, they laughed loudly to hear how Maddock had chased the wrong game. But Maddock hurried back to the orchard and, without asking permission, entered the Queen's tent.

"What cowards you have for lovers, you light ladies!" he taunted them. "By Saint Nectan, I chased them half way to Rome and they would not stop to fight me however much I shamed them with foul names. By Heaven, ladies, your lovers are hares. They run so fast that they do not know what honour is."

Though Isolt had no doubt of Tristan's courage, she did not contradict Maddock's lying boast, for she would not admit that a man had visited her. "I don't know what you're talking about," she said crossly. But Bronwen was so humiliated by the accusation that she had given her love to a coward that she replied angrily, "God grant me patience! No warrior would run away from you, Lord Maddock. Who were those mighty men whom you claim that you hunted from our wood? Or were they shepherds armed with hazel sticks? What badges and colours did they bear? Let us hear who those brave men were, so that we can beware of their boasting if we should ever be so unlucky as to meet them."

"By Saint Nectan, one of them fled so fast that I could not even see his badge but he had a copper shield. The other had a gilded shield, adorned with green leaves. It was a shield which I do not know so I think that its owner must have been a foreigner."

"By my hope of salvation, if I meet any man who bears such a shield, I shall spit in his eye. Thank you for warning me," Bronwen said stiffly, and turned her back. But, when she was alone with Isolt, she spilled the anger from her heart.

"Unlucky for me the day, when I came with you to Cornwall!" said Bronwen. "For your sake I gave up my family and friends, my homeland, my chance of marriage and for your sake, I sacrificed my maidenhead in your marriage-bed. But you have repaid me ill. Once you tried to have me killed and now you have succeeded in tricking me into taking a coward to my bed. You and Tristan shamed me, in order to bring me down to your own vile level. But I shall not let you trick me again, Lady Isolt."

"Ah! God! You and Cardin have made a plot," Isolt accused her. "You want to go with him and you are seeking some excuse to leave my service. Don't leave me alone in a foreign land, you traitor. Remember your promise to my mother, Bronwen."

"Indeed, Lady, it is time that I paid more attention to that promise" Bronwen answered sternly. "I have no intention of leaving you. No! I shall stick to your side and I shall do just what your mother asked me to do; I shall guard your honour. May my soul rot in hell, if I ever let Tristan come near you again!"

In various disguises Tristan and Cardin tried to gain admission to their ladies but, whatever they did, they were unsuccessful. For Bronwen's hatred was daily sharpened by Maddock's loud boasting in the court and she guarded Isolt closely. Cardin soon grew tired of the devious plots and undignified disguises and he decided to make a pilgrimage to Saint Michael's Mount and rejoin Tristan later. But Tristan was too upset to worry about his honour. He did not understand why no message came from Isolt and he was afraid that she might be in danger because of Maddock.

Tristan resolved to change his appearance so that not even Isolt would easily recognise him. He bound pieces of wood behind his knees, so that his legs were always bent and he rolled in nettles and smeared himself with dock-leaves, until his skin was puffed and blotchy. Then he dressed himself in filthy rags and carried the wooden bowl which Isolt had given him at Cardiff. Tristan, bent and hobbling like a crippled beggar, waited near the church at Mass-time. The King's servants pushed him aside and some of the guards hit him with their spears, but still he begged, and tapped his wooden bowl under the courtiers' noses.

Tristan hoped that, when the ladies came by, either Isolt or Bronwen would recognise his bowl and arrange a meeting but, although he beat his bowl to attract their attention, they were both so deep in bitter thought that neither of them looked at his bowl. The lords and ladies went into church and knelt down to hear Mass, but desperate Tristan pushed in after them, and in spite of the rough handling by the Queen's servants, he held his bowl towards Isolt and whispered urgently, "Alms, sweet Queen! In God's name, give me alms. My life is at an end, unless you help me, Lady."

Isolt looked up angrily and after a glance at the beggar's hideous face she looked at his bowl. She recognised the bowl and with this clue she discovered Tristan in the grotesque beggar. Her mouth opened and shut with shock and terror. She feared that Bronwen might betray Tristan to King Mark's vengeance and she did not know how to speak to Tristan without the knowledge of Bronwen at her side. Carefully she slipped a ring from her finger and turned to a page standing behind her. "Give the beggar this ring and tell him to come to my hall for a meal," she whispered.

But Bronwen saw the ring; she saw the beggar's bowl and she recognised Tristan. "You are too generous to such a vile man," she told Isolt harshly. She seized the ring and she ordered the guards to drag the beggar from the church and to thrash him if he returned.

Then at last Tristan knew why he had been unable to get word to Isolt; he realised that Bronwen had turned against him. Throughout their love-life Tristan and Isolt had depended on Bronwen's help. Without her consent they could never have met and they had no hope of meeting again now that their friend had become their enemy.

Tristan was desolate, because he would never be able to speak to Isolt, but in order to be as near her as possible, he crept into the palace and hid himself under the wooden steps outside an old grain-store. Tristan had been suffering such hunger and torment that his body was weak and his spirit too had been utterly broken by his discovery of Bronwen's hatred. So he rolled himself up in his beggar's rags and gave himself over to death.

That evening Huden, Isolt's old hound, who once had belonged to Tristan, caught the scent of his former master and, whining eagerly, followed his nose to the granary stairs. The kennelman called the hound away but Huden was licking Tristan's face and would not budge. The handler therefore crawled under the stairs, to see what Huden had found. This handler had been in Tristan's service and he recognised the bowl in the beggar's hands. He ran and told the Queen, "Gracious Lady, Huden has found a dying man with the Lord Tristan's favourite drinking-bowl."

Then Isolt begged Bronwen: "Have mercy on Tristan. You used to love him and held him in high honour. Please go and comfort him, and if you still refuse to let him come to me, at least tell him why."

Bronwen went to the granary and upbraided Tristan for tricking her into granting her love to a worthless coward. "For Cardin," she said, "had not even pluck enough to stand up to Maddock." But Tristan assured her that Maddock had never met Cardin himself and he explained how the squires had lured Maddock away from the orchard to protect their masters and their masters' ladies. Finally he undertook that Cardin would avenge her for the public shame which she had suffered because of Maddock's boasting in the court.

Then Bronwen relented and she told the porter to carry the sick man into the women's hall so that he could be nursed back to health. With Isolt's medical skill and inspiring love Tristan soon became well enough to travel and Bronwen sent him to fetch Cardin.

Tristan told Cardin that Maddock had boasted of routing a warrior whose badge was a wreath of leaves on a golden shield and he said that Bronwen required Cardin to prove his prowess by conquering Maddock publicly in battle.

When Cardin heard about Maddock's boasting, he was furious and his chance for revenge came on May Morning, for the May-day sports were open to all comers and no warrior could refuse a challenge without dishonour. To begin with, Cardin distinguished himself in the athletic games. Then he armed himself and confronted Maddock. He held up his shield and shouted for all to hear, "Cowardly Maddock, here before you stands the warrior with the golden shield and the badge of leaves whom you boasted that you had chased half-way to Rome. In the presence of those who have heard your boast, I defy you to prove it."

Maddock was reluctant to take up the challenge but he truly thought that this man had run away from him once, and when his friends reminded him of his honour, he armed himself to defend it. Maddock was strong and well-built but he had no heart for pain or danger so when he discovered that Cardin was a fierce and skilful fighter, he tried to buy him off. Maddock offered Cardin generous compensation, but Cardin had come to the May Games for only one thing, Maddock's death. After calling him "coward" and "caitiff" with every blow, he got what he came for. He cut off Maddock's head and offered it to Bronwen on the point of his spear.

Cardin's triumph was short-lived, for Maddock's kinsmen gathered in arms to avenge his death. Tristan and Cardin had to fight their way to their horses and they had to ride like a pair of roe-deer with the hunt after them, twisting and turning through forest paths and unfrequented ways, to reach their ship alive. After all the weary weeks of deception and devices, they had obtained only a few hours of the love for which they had come so far. As they sailed away, they could claim only one achievement — the hated Maddock's death.

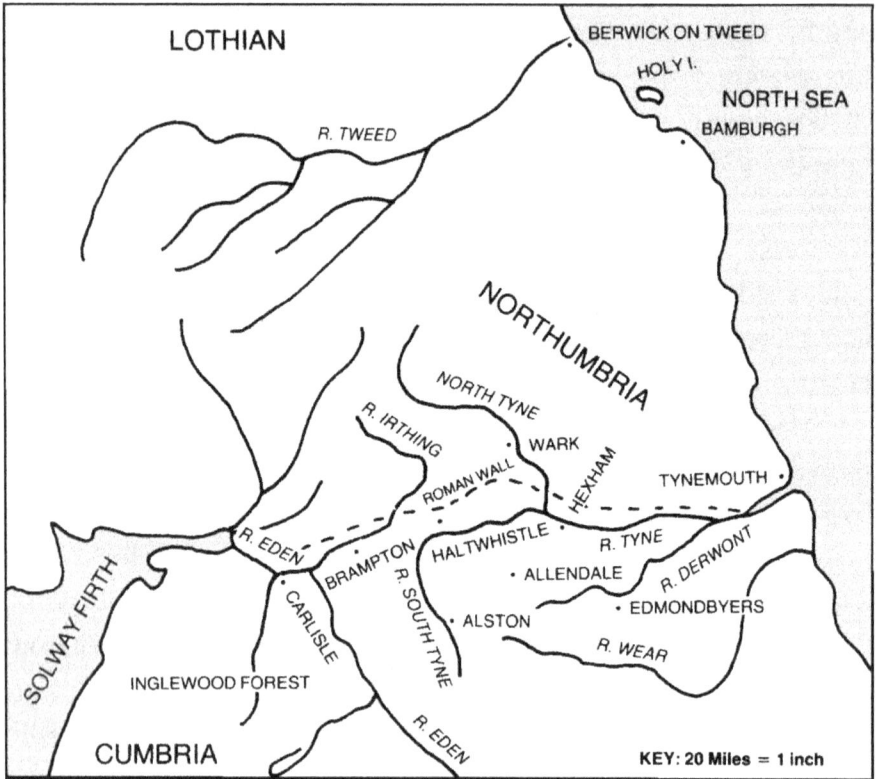

CHAPTER 21

JOURNEY'S END IN LOVERS' MEETING

Back in Cumbria, Tristan and Cardin hunted in Inglewood by day and in the evenings sat with Isolt Whitehands, while Tristan sang songs about Isolt. When Isolt Whitehands lay beside Tristan in bed, she desired his love ever more urgently, but he still refused her, and at last, she suspected that he was cheating her. Isolt Whitehands had begun to doubt Tristan's story of a wound as she had heard rumours of his love affair in Cornwall.

Behind Tristan's back people began to call him 'Tristan the Lover" and one afternoon, when he was riding home, from hunting in Inglewood, a large and well-armed man galloped up and asked: "Do you know where Tristan the Lover is? They say in the town that he is hunting in this locality."

"Why do you want Tristan? Who are you?" Tristan asked sharply, but he added with a smile, "You need not fear to waste your breath in telling me everything, for I am Tristan."

"Thanks be to God!" the stranger cried. "I also, Lord, am Tristan. 'Little Tristan' they call me in fun, because I am so large. I have come for your help, Lord Tristan.

"Two days ago English robbers raided my farm at Alston, while I was out hunting. They drove off my cattle and stole away my newly wedded bride. I tracked the raiders to the stockade of 'Bragging

Athulf at Edmondbyers and I heard that Athulf is keeping my sweet bride to be his concubine. Help me to get her back, Lord Tristan. By your fame as a lover, go with me to Edmondbyers, before it is too late."

"You shall have my help, friend Tristan. Come back to Carlisle with me tonight, while I gather my friends. Then we will come with you into Northumberland tomorrow."

"By my oath, namesake," Little Tristan protested, "your reputation as a lover is much exaggerated, if you think that I can wait so long before rescuing my lady. Sir, by the great love which, I hear, you suffer for the Queen of Cornwall, come with me tonight."

"Ah, friend Tristan! When you speak of the love which I 'suffer', I know that you are a lover who deserves help, for only a true lover would think of 'suffering' love. For the sake of that great love which I suffer, I will ride with you now but we must wait at Alston for my squire to bring me my arms and armour and a fresh horse. Even for a true lover I am not willing to go into enemy territory with only my hunting sword to defend me."

The two Tristans spent the night at Alston and early in the morning they rode over the fells and down the valley of the Northumbrian River Derwent. Not far from Edmondbyers they came upon two English hunters. "These are two of Athulf's four brothers," Little Tristan said, so the Tristans attacked and killed them. But the hunters had sounded their horns, to call their brothers from their hall, and soon the Tristans had to deal with two more well-armed warriors plus a gang of peasants. The battle was fierce, and in less than an hour, Athulf and all his brothers were dead. But Little Tristan was dead as well and Tristan the Lover was badly wounded in the left arm.

Tristan mounted with difficulty and made his way homewards as quickly as he could, for he was nearly twenty miles inside enemy territory. His arm throbbed and swelled like a football and he was dizzy and faint. But his horse carried him faithfully and he reached Carlisle on the following day.

Tristan's squire related in the palace how Little Tristan had called his master "Tristan the Lover" and had appealed for his help "by the great love which you suffer for the Queen of Cornwall." When Isolt Whitehands heard it, she thought bitterly of her loveless marriage. But she did her wifely duty and called the healers, and she nursed her lord as well as she could.

In spite of the care of Isolt and the healers, Tristan got worse. The healers bruised leaves and pounded roots. They stewed herbs and bought famous cures from foreign merchants. They bound Tristan's wound in this sort of plaster and that sort of bandage. Nevertheless, the poison would not yield to any of their remedies. Tristan's arm grew black; his whole body swelled and ached and his wound stank with ever-running pus.

Tristan was dying and he remembered that only the great skill of the Queen of Leinster had cured him when he had been wounded by Morolt's poisoned sword. He was too weak to travel to Ireland but he knew that his lover, Isolt Fairhair, had great skill in medicine and he resolved to seek her help. Tristan asked Cardin to visit him, and when his friend had come, he ordered everybody else, including his wife, to leave the hut where he lay. Tristan propped himself up on one elbow and leant against the wall. "My friend," said Tristan, "you are my only ally in this country, where I am far from my family and countrymen. I rely on you to help me in my need, for I am poisoned and I shall certainly die within six weeks or so, unless help reaches me. The only person in the whole world who can help me is the Queen of Cornwall, for she knows the remedies for all the poisons used in Britain and the lands of the North. I am too weak to undertake a sea-voyage and have too many enemies at the Cornish court to go there safely. Therefore I depend on you to fetch that good healer. Will you be my messenger?"

"By all means, companion!" Cardin answered at once. "I would gladly risk death, in order to save your life. Tell me your message and I will take it to her as quickly as I can."

"Thank you, dear friend. Take this ring, which is a love-token between Queen Isolt and me, and visit the court of the King of Cornwall, as though you were a merchant selling cloth. Show the Queen your cloth and, in doing so, let her see this ring. Then leave it to her to arrange a private conversation, for only she knows who her enemies are.

"When you are alone with the Queen, say to her, 'Tristan sends his love and service; he sends the greetings of a lover to his lady. He has sent me to you, because he needs your help so urgently that he will surely die if you do not help him. Your lover, Tristan, has been wounded with a poisoned Northumbrian weapon and no healer can be found who knows the remedy for that poison. Tristan is always in pain; he stinks like a cesspit and he is already too weak to get out of bed. You, Gracious Lady, are the only healer who knows the remedies for all the poisons, and Tristan begs you to help him.'

"Then remind my lady of the great love which we enjoyed together and remind her of the great griefs which we suffered together and remind her that because of our love I have lost both the trust of my uncle, King Mark, and the inheritance of the Kingdom of Cornwall. Say to her, good Cardin: 'Tristan bids you to remember the loving-cup which you shared, and he bids you to remember how you gave him this ring as a pledge of your undying love when he parted from you. Tristan has never loved any other woman except you, Fair Isolt and even his wife is still a virgin because he loves only you. Now, Isolt Fairhair, prove that you also love Tristan. Come to his help at once; or he will be beyond help. This ring which you gave Tristan he now gives back to you as a keepsake for, whether you come to him as he asks or leave him to his fate, he will not need it for any more messengers."

Tristan wept at the sad memories which his message recalled and Cardin beside him also wept for pity. But another person listened through the wall and there was no pity in <u>that</u> person's heart.

"There is one thing more," Tristan told Cardin. "I cannot be sure of living any longer than six weeks, unless my healer comes. Therefore make haste and bring the lovely lady back within that time. And Cardin! Hoist a white sail, if you bring my healer but hoist a black sail, if you return without her."

Cardin sailed away on his secret mission and Tristan lay on his bed, daily becoming weaker. At first he asked to be lifted up, so that he could study every ship which came up the river but later on he became too weak to watch the river himself and his wife kept watch on his behalf. He was so frail that only his brave spirit kept him alive and his spirit lived only on hope.

The fifth week followed the fourth and the seven days of the sixth week passed one by one in stormy winds and rain. No ship could sail up the Solway Firth in such weather and Tristan clenched his fists, gritted his teeth and held onto his fleeing life for a few more days, hoping that better weather would bring his lover in. On the day after the storm several ships came sailing up the River Eden and Tristan commanded Isolt Whitehands to watch them carefully and to tell him at once when she saw Cardin's ship.

The hours drifted away and the tension in the hut grew brittle. Tristan waited on his bed and Isolt Whitehands waited at the window. Suddenly Isolt Whitehands jumped from her seat and her face was strangely twisted, as though she suffered some internal pain. "I can see Cardin's ship. I recognise it," she said. Then she added in a fierce whisper, "And the sail is <u>black</u>."

Tristan gasped, as though he had been hit in the belly. "No, no! " Surely the sail is white?" he pleaded. "I told Cardin to hoist a <u>white</u>

sail." Isolt Whitehands came and stood over Tristan. "No!" she said harshly. "The sail is <u>black.</u>"

Tristan groaned and turned his face to the wall. He did not see the hatred on his wife's face, for he was thinking only of his lover. "God save Isolt and me!" he murmured. "I die for lack of your help, dear love. At least pity me in death."

"Die, you deceiver. Die, you cheat," Isolt Whitehands hissed. "You left your wife a frustrated virgin because of your love for the Queen of Cornwall. I heard you say it, heard you through the wall. For the sake of another man's wife, you wicked wretch, you left your own wife unloved and discontented. But I spared you, Tristan, until I saw Cardin's sail. That condemned you to death, for I would rather be an honoured widow standing beside your grave than a dishonoured wife turned out of your house by a Cornish concubine."

Tristan heard not a word of his wife's venom, for his head was buzzing. He whispered, "Dearest Isolt! Dearest Isolt! Dearest Isolt!" Then "<u>Isolt!</u>" he cried aloud - and died.

Slowly, slowly up the winding river Cardin's ship gybed and tacked, as she ran before a fickle wind. But at last the seamen ran their ship aground below the city walls, furled the white sail on its spar and put the gangplank out. Cardin and Isolt Fairhair ran eagerly ashore. They lifted up their heads to listen and Isolt asked an old man standing on the shore, "What is the meaning of those bells? Why are the townspeople wailing so mournfully?"

"Lady, we mourn the passing of our good friend, the gallant Lord Tristan, who saved us from the English. He died this morning, only an hour ago and they have just taken his dear body to lie in the great church, so that all who loved him may pay their last respects."

Isolt said nothing but picked up her skirts and ran up the street towards the church. When the townspeople saw Isolt's face, they stopped their wailing and gaped in wonder, for never had they seen such beauty nor such grief and, when Isolt entered the church, the mourners instinctively stepped back from Tristan's bier. She walked firmly forward, until she looked down at her lover's face.

"Ah, Tristan!" she said. "Now that I see you dead, my life has no purpose. If I had come just a little sooner, I could have healed you and we could have talked of our love together and we could have had joy and pleasure again. But, since I am too late to heal you, I shall die with you for we have shared great rapture and delight and we have shared great pain and sorrow. Whatever strength there has been in my life has been there because of our love and, now that our love is dead, I am too weak to live any longer."

Isolt kissed Tristan's cold lips; she laid her cheek on his and her breast on his and her legs on his. Face to face and body to body she embraced him and held him as close as she could.

"Tristan! Dearest Tristan!" she whispered and with those words she gave up her life.

King Mark had pursued his wife and his ship reached port not long after hers. Angrily he strode into the church but, when he saw her dead on Tristan's bier, his anger turned to tears.

"God have mercy on their souls!" he cried, and when he had heard the whole love-story of Tristan and Isolt, from the accident of the love-potion to the vengeance of the jealous wife, he said, "Ah, Tristan, my dear, dear friend! If only I had known! If only you had told me on your return from Ireland that you were in love with Isolt, my betrothed, you could have had her for your bride and Cornwall for your heritage."

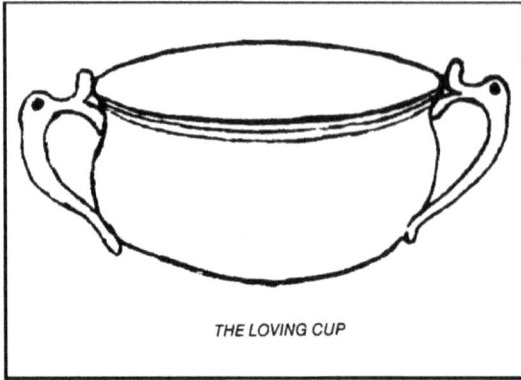

THE LOVING CUP

The End.

Thankyou for reading "TRISTAN THE LOVER".

I am very interested in your thoughts and comments, so please review this book on the Amazon website.

1) Search –*Tristan the Lover*
2) Scroll down to *'Write a customer review'* button.

Or you can Email me at: ianfraser@sifipublishing.co.uk

Many thanks,
Ian Fraser.

ABOUT THE AUTHOR

Ian Fraser was born into a well-known Scottish family, of which practically every man for more than seven hundred years had been a warrior. But, because his father was disinherited for choosing the 'cowardly' profession of clergyman, the author was brought up and educated in southern England. He has an Oxford Master degree in Modern History and since his student days has immersed himself in medieval history. During the war he was an officer in the Royal Navy (actually a 'torpedo pilot' in the Fleet Air Arm) and in 1943 both decorated with the Distinguished Service Cross and captured. After two + years as a German P.O. W., he became an administrator in the British Colonial Service, working primarily in Malaysia and Singapore. There, he met and worked amongst simple people, comparable to our ancestors of a thousand years ago. He was deeply impressed by how vastly different human beings are in different times and places and by the fallacy of the assumption that all men are, and always have been, the same. He was honoured as an Officer of the Order of the British Empire in 1960 and later served in Aden and the Bahamas.

.

Also by Ian Fraser

THE KING-BORN

Few of us in the English speaking world nowadays believe that a man is bound by destiny, but medieval Europeans had no doubt of it. A "lucky" man would be successful and an" ill starred" man would fail. The gods were paramount, as is shown in *THE KING BORN*.

During the twelfth to fourteenth centuries, the story of Olaf the Strong was a favourite of the English minstrels. Olaf was the son of Magnus, King of the Danes but when Magnus died of his wounds while his son was still too young to hold the throne, Magnus' brother, Thorard, was greedy and plotted to kill Olaf. However, by the will of the gods, Olaf overcame all obstacles and eventually gained not only the throne of Denmark but the throne of England as well.

THE KING BORN may be an old English myth of the Danish conquest of England in 1013 A.D. but it provides a fascinating glimpse of Northern Europe a thousand years ago as well as the excitement of following Olaf's adventures.

Available in paperback and Ebook on Amazon
and at other retailers

THE STRANGER WARRIOR

This is an exciting historical tale for older children based on a famous British legend, with the background of life in the British Isles in about 900A.D. as full and accurate as present knowledge allows.

The hero, Horn, is orphaned and cast adrift when a Viking fleet conquers the Isle of Man for the King of Norway. Because Horn has neither land nor treasure, he pursues his sacred duty of revenge by striving to become a famous warrior. He serves both an English elderman and an Irish king, rejecting comfort and love in his search for fame At last, after many battles he avenges his father, reconquers the Isle of Man and – almost incidentally – collects a bride.

To be published by sifipublishing in Summer 2013.

www.sifipublishing.co.uk